Volume I

Adventure in Meditation
Spirituality for the 21st Century

by
Carol E. Parrish-Harra, Ph.D.

SPARROW HAWK PRESS
TAHLEQUAH, OKLAHOMA

Library of Congress Cataloging-in-Publication Data
Parrish-Harra, Carol E.
Adventure in Meditation Vol. I: Spirituality for the 21st Century
    A course in meditation presenting psycho-spiritual technologies to aid practitioners in living more consciously, leading to higher awareness and soul infusion. Tutoring available. Includes ageless wisdom teachings and tools for overcoming barriers to individual growth.

ISBN No. 0-945027-13-3: $17.95
1. Meditation—tutoring available, 2. Spirituality, 3. Ageless wisdom teachings, 4. Psycho-spiritual technologies, 5. Agni Yoga teachings, 6. Bibliography.

Library of Congress Catalog Card Number
95-71835

Manufactured in the United States of America

Dedicated to
the Inner Teachers of humanity
who have guided many to the Light

Volume I Contents

Editor's Note. An asterisk indicates terms which may be new to some readers, terms which will be found in *The New Dictionary of Spiritual Thought* by Carol E. Parrish-Harra (Sparrow Hawk Press, 1994), a companion volume of 1100 words, concepts, and symbols helpful to the present work. The asterisk is used only with the first appearance of the most unfamiliar words to minimize distraction. *The New Dictionary of Spiritual Thought* contains terms and concepts related to spiritual sciences, esoteric Christianity, astrology, metaphysics, ageless wisdom teachings, and more. Available from Sparrow Hawk Press, Sparrow Hawk Village, 11 Summit Ridge Dr., Tahlequah, OK 74464, 918-456-3421 or 1-800-386-7161. $14.95 plus $2 shipping/handling.

Most biblical references are taken from the King James Version or the Peshitta Bible, the classic version of the Holy Bible as translated from the Aramaic (Syriac) text—the language of Jesus—by renowned scholar George M. Lamsa.

Volume I List of Figures

Introduction

In the time of oral traditions, a knowledgeable one, somewhere in the world and in every age, assisted spiritual seekers to progress along the way of their own spiritual path. We have sought to duplicate this approach as much as possible. Thus, it is my pleasure to encourage the use of these lessons for individual spiritual growth. It is my wish, as well, to lend a personal touch and, with our tutors, provide a modern version of discipleship training. Mentoring is a way of contributing one's experience to enrich an already successful course. Clearly defined spiritual technologies guide away from the ambiguities that inevitably arise from random reading toward a more contemporary, cohesive, and expanded comprehension of the eternal mysteries.

Meditation needs to be recognized as the primary tool for aware, creative aspirants as we move into the twenty-first century. This course has been designed for those wanting guidance in dependable techniques for transformation through meditation. For those serious about transformation, complete involvement is the way of choice. Meditation expands horizons, and diligence in dissolving barriers hastens the process. The eclectic teachings herein respect spiritual heritages and meditation systems of both East and West, and we strongly urge you—whatever your tradition and background—to study, persist, and put into practice these teachings.

Since meditation creates a foundation for both inner knowing and revelation, the seeker needs a mentor to whom he or she may turn when help is needed. Knowing the value of interacting with a guide as consciousness expands, Sancta Sophia Seminary offers trained tutors to perform this service. Correspondence with your tutor may concern questions about lesson content or procedures, reactions to what you are asked to do, the sharing of meaningful experiences, valuative statements concerning the lessons, or problems you experience with meditation—anything you feel may be useful to your progress or that you wish to convey. We encourage you to consider inner exploration with a guide; active participation provides motivation and will help you avoid pitfalls—as well as adding pizzazz!

The vastness of meditation experiences, as well as divine discontent, impels us to venture inward. Spiritually dedicated, piece by piece, we discover who we are. Since the very process of life is designed to excite us and develop inner awareness, each new experience inspires greater interest in a "knowing" that satisfies the soul.

Our techniques are presented in three volumes. These three volumes clarify the processes of meditation and the levels to be explored. They also provide direction in effective techniques to diminish barriers and enhance dynamic living. We employ seed thoughts as offered in the modern philosophy of *Agni Yoga (ethical living) to hasten the illumination process. Agni—meaning "fire," a symbol of purification significant to all spiritual persuasions—burns away distortion and guides us to the inner reality.

Meditation transforms lives, and as our levels of understanding advance, so too will our meditation. To pierce the veil is our challenge and our reward. To know the light of Christ with our whole being is our great goal. Each flash affirms the existence of more; each rewarding experience encourages. To try too hard blocks us; to do too little discourages our spirit.

Undertake these lessons prepared to contact the presence of the honorable teacher within who awaits the opportunity to stir you. As you advance, with proper attention and attitude, more will be revealed than the words on the page. Your Inner Presence will respond and lead you. You will reconnect with the wisdom of the past, and having recollected, contemplated, and reassembled your awareness, you will encounter your true self.

Open the door gently, dear friend, and enter into the light, one step at a time.

From the Author

I n this course I offer the spiritual awareness and meditation experience gathered and integrated through years of personal practice and instruction, having been a serious student of the wisdom tradition since 1965.

A near-death experience changed my life and catapulted me to my mission. Standing in that Presence of Light, profound love and incredible awareness were etched into my mind. I knew it was mine to pass on. Returning to a world bereft of such awareness (1958), I struggled alone, beseeching a teacher. Gradually I learned to sit quietly and allow the Light to return, to love me, and, in due time, to teach me. I did not even know the word "meditation," but I soon discovered the wonder and reward of that experience. Then and now, my inner connection bestows a treasure of wisdom and love to my life. My commitment is to engender and encourage this in others.

This guide is prepared for those now ready. To respect the lineage of one's path is necessary, so I pass to you who enter these gates the treasures I have received. I have been blessed to experience individual instruction over many years with three remarkable and wise teachers. In practices of the past, disciples met one-on-one with a mentor who instructed, disciplined, and challenged them to confront the obstructions to their spiritual growth. Whether or not student and teacher liked one another was unimportant. If they embraced spiritually, they soon realized a long-term commitment to a relationship of karmic dimensions had been entered. The honor of each was pledged.

As we move into the Aquarian age, the tradition of personal relationships between teacher and disciple which existed over the centuries seems to be vanishing, but it remains as a foundation stone on our path. At the end of the Piscean age, a large part of humanity appears ready to move from child of God to coworker with God, participating in a planetary blueprint and learning to work cooperatively in groups rather than as the solitary travelers of the past. Training in the transitional period may be likened to building a bridge to connect two dissimilar terrains. Some are ready to know what the hand-trained of the past were given so it will not be lost and these necessary concepts may be integrated to convey certain keys to those who seek to follow.

With what attitude do we approach the teachings? With quiet heart and mind, listening carefully. It is with hunger that we seek to discover our true nature, and it is the soul that teaches. It is through our meditation experiences that we awaken, perceive, and know. I want to excite you about the practice of meditation because I believe as the ancients believed: Meditation is a portal behind which the soul awaits. The Inner Teacher eagerly anticipates your presence, *for now we see darkly, but then we shall see face to face.*

In Special Recognition

T his work began as a set of meditation lessons designed for Sancta Sophia *(Holy Wisdom)* Seminary, the educational institute for Light of Christ Community Church, a modern mystical Christian church, esoteric in understanding.

The challenge of preparing such a course was accepted by two diligent workers, the Reverends Stanley and Helen Ainsworth, and they have again cooperated generously in the rewrite for this series.

Prior to ministry, Rev. Stanley Ainsworth retired from a career as an educator. The author of *Positive Emotional Power,* he enjoys writing and speaking about transformation techniques. Rev. Helen Ainsworth has written articles for magazines and religious publications, as well as radio copy, for many years.

In the early 1970s, the Ainsworths participated in extensive studies with Roy Eugene Davis at the Center for Spiritual Awareness. After retiring in 1975, they came to Florida to pursue their interest in spiritual themes. They prepared for ministry with me, blending the psychological and spiritual interests of a lifetime into service. In 1982, Stanley and Helen began to write our meditation course, lesson by lesson. A committee of tutors—experienced, astute meditators—volunteered to respond to student correspondence letter by letter. Seminary students welcomed the written study and delighted in personal feedback. Soon people not formally in the seminary program wanted the lessons as well. Enthusiasm grew. Today tutors continue to nurture students, and this mentoring greatly enhances many lives.

Carol E. Parrish-Harra

From the Reverends
Stanley and Helen Ainsworth

As part of the early seminary, we thoroughly enjoyed working with the many gifted and enthusiastic students over the years. We began to talk with Carol about publishing the lessons with greater input from her.

During the process, Sancta Sophia Seminary greatly expanded its program. Now the need became more apparent for an even broader emphasis on the benefits of meditation and the contribution it brings. We are particularly pleased that this course and the assistance of the tutors will be available to others not formally enrolled in the seminary. We were asked to coauthor the new material. After editing and the addition of new topics, we saw that the current material was largely a product of Carol's creativity and felt she should be sole author. The bulk of the text we initially prepared is included in this expanded version. We appreciate the gratitude many students have expressed as they complete this vital segment of their studies.

This is a unique compilation. We do not believe you will find another that contains such a wide spectrum of topics, information, and ideas for personal growth and spiritual practices. We are sure it will be useful to you long after you have completed formal studies. Enjoy!

Sparrow Hawk Village
December, 1992

Acknowledgements

An expression of my heartfelt gratitude must go to the meditation tutors who have served students and Sancta Sophia Seminary faithfully and anonymously through the years. They are most sincerely dedicated to the lives they touch.

I wish to applaud, as well, the students of meditation who made the earlier lessons popular and encouraged this more extensive work.

And a salute of special appreciation to my coworkers for the diligence and extra efforts each one generously made as the lessons traveled toward completion. Thank you also for your good humor as we met deadline after deadline. Blessings to each of you—especially to Mary Beth Marvin for her editorial expertise, skillful critiquing, and design concepts; to Norma Hallstrom for her editorial assistance to Mary Beth, her dedicated research, and for sharing her own personal progress as she worked on the manuscript; to Marianne Sansing who combined computer skills and design and illustration talents to satisfy my desire to create a book that is interesting to look at, even as it is about a subject hard to illustrate; and to a new student in the seminary's prep program, Nell Thalasinos of Sunset Beach, North Carolina, for her outstanding cover design. Nell and I chatted about the book and the cover while she was taking classes. When she returned home, she made it happen.

An additional thank you to the many whose help was given in the numerous steps we took together between the time this project began—almost six years ago—and its publication. Let us rejoice in a task well done.

The Pyramid of
Meditation Development

Introducing the Pyramid of Meditation Development

Our journey begins at the base as we contemplate the choice and commit ourselves to the ascent. Each level includes a skill to build, a work to do, and a result—all leading to the desired evolution of consciousness. Each level presents its challenge as we build inner tools with which to know anew.

Level 1.   Here we master relaxation and centering to escape the distractions and domination of the body. (Lessons 1 and 2, volume 1.)

Level 2.   Passive meditation stimulates the inner senses and teaches receptivity to High Self's impressions. Here exists guidance for the personality level of life and the building of the cup in which impressions are caught. Purification work is begun through passive techniques designed to exercise inner senses and to provide training for the spiritual practitioner. Purification heals and helps all of humanity, as well as the disciple. (Lessons 3-7, volume 1.)

Level 3.   Will is the necessary constituent of this level. The cup built by passive meditation is in place. Now active meditation begins inner focus; the focused mind pierces the veil and accumulates information vibrating to the keynote or seed thought. As we break through into the Cloud of Knowable Things, the cup collects the precipitation and organizes it into understandable and usable ideas. (Lessons 8, 9, and volume 2.)

Level 4.   Purification of ego is the primary work as one approaches soul infusion. The miasma created by old thoughtforms and personality's strong desire currents forms clouds that distort the wisdom gleaned from the light of the Soul. Here we confront the shadows. We consciously intensify clearing in order to embrace wisdom. (Volumes 2 and 3.)

Level 5.   Soul alignment is our great goal. As meditation practices are established in the personal life, the human soul ascends toward its true purpose. *Remember, ye are Gods.* Soul-alignment meditations guide the initiate—personality and soul—into right relationship . . . into Enlightenment. (Volume 3: Hurrah, we reach the summit!)

Meditation is truly a doorway to the world of spiritual realities. Your progress depends upon you. Embrace the quest!

SOUL

Temple of the Soul

Level 5 — **Goal: Soul Alignment** — *Vol. III*
Completing the Task:
Integration of Human and Divine
Vol. III: emphasizes the work of soul energies

Level 4 — **Dissolve Barriers to Hasten Growth** — *Vols. II & III*
Intensify Purification and Build Virtues
Vols. II & III: clear miasma and experience more light

Level 3 — **Active Meditation and Advanced Concepts** — *Vol. I*
Work As If: "I Am the Soul"
Lessons 8–9: gain new awareness; touch the inner teacher

Level 2 — **Passive Meditation and Specific Work Techniques** — *Vol. I*
Building the Cup—High-Self Contacts
Lessons 3–7: build tools to access your inner hidden resources

Level 1 — **Basic Technologies Create the Transformative Foundation** — *Vol. I*
Relaxation and Centering Most Important
Lessons 1–2: know humanity's process and create a solid foundation for your inner life

Figure i. The Pyramid of Meditation Development.

The Great Goal

Meditation is the science of God-realization.
It is the most practical science in the world.
Most people would want to meditate if they
understood its value and experienced
its beneficial effects.

—Paramahansa Yogananda
Metaphysical Meditations

M editation stands as the single most important discipline recommended to help attain self-realization and oneness with the Infinite. Other activities, such as study, right-living, appropriate utilization of the body and emotions, as well as procedures for concentration, are seen as preliminary and preparatory disciplines. Meditation, in one form or another, is an ever-evolving process for reaching total awareness. It is a key to unlock the aspect of self so often obscured in our daily lives. As Torkom Saraydarian states, "It is impossible to live the path of discipleship and *initiation without meditation."[1] Thus, for the serious student of truths, meditation becomes the core process.

We live in a time rich in promise; information continues to emerge to guide and assist humanity to fulfill its divine destiny. Self-mastery, self-actualization, and illumination are terms which acknowledge humanity's innate, glorious nature. While methods differ in various cultures and time periods, there have always existed individuals who envision the future and lead the way. All guides to transformation declare meditation is the decisive factor.

Today we stand poised for a leap forward. Many believe the mind-stuff of humanity is disciplined and trained sufficiently to realize new capabilities; wise ones disagree. Brain development and meditation techniques combine to unfold human potential. Formerly, *mystery schools and temples provided guidelines and disciplines upon which to build a stable foundation for those who sought illumination. But many of the ancient techniques have been forgotten. Few today realize we must recapitulate past awareness and integrate our psycho-spiritual nature. These lessons assist in recollecting past skills and in learning to penetrate the *Cloud of Knowable Things. Having taught meditation and transformation techniques for nearly thirty years, I am eager to share.

Enlightened effort ignites transformation which manifests in psychological clearing and beneficial change. In these lessons you are asked to embrace disciplines and procedures as introduced and put them into ongoing practice. This is our way of conveying the necessity to ritualistically perform what are considered essential steps to foster the state of altered consciousness we call Oneness with Divinity. Those dedicated to a path of disciplined creativity witness to such metamorphosis.

Four major practices acknowledged by all traditions for those seeking enlightenment are:

1. Reading and hearing about God, talking and listening to God. We call this meditation and prayer practices.

2. Keeping company with others similarly spiritually focused. This happens naturally because we enjoy the vibrations and stimulation of our like-minded friends—birds of a feather flock together.

3. Leading virtuous lifestyles. Putting our code of ethics into practice affirms self-esteem. Doing to others as we would have them do to us encourages us to learn experientially. Honorable people, by nature, accord others more personal freedom.

4. Contemplating the ramifications of spiritual laws as we grow in our understanding of them.

In meditation, a process of placing our mind in harmony with the Great Mind, we discover ever-expanding new growth and development of our human capabilities. Just as we acknowledge the fetus recapitulates the development of the animal kingdom, I suggest humanity recapitulates its building of the human mind, its mental capabilities. Spiritual disciplines preserve a heritage of experience for the aspirants of today. Wisdom suggests we begin with simple techniques and gradually advance to the more sophisticated so that wherever we have weak areas, under-developed skill, or "unfinished effort," our practice will build a foundation for strengthening and change. Recapitulation is little understood outside the teachings of ancient wisdom where evolution—individual and collective—is quite respected.

Early beings of caveman consciousness lived by their instinctual nature. Self-consciousness emerged at the time of *individuation. Since then, humanity (the fourth kingdom) has continued to evolve step by step toward the creation of the fifth kingdom, the kingdom of souls.[2] Just as a magnificent leap forward occurred when the human kingdom separated from the animal, we will experience this kind of acceleration to new capabilities when the imminent initiation is achieved.

Think this way, please. Part of humanity is in fact surging forward, exploring and stretching into expansion of consciousness. Those who do so experience, comprehend, and attempt to share their explorations with others. New understanding is evident in many areas. Consider the physicists and the new sciences of space. Inventors tell of ideas given them or first perceived as they dreamed. Think of the new math that challenges many, or computer science, so easy for some to grasp but a great stretch for others. We label people "creative" when they relate in art, music, or drama in ways the majority does not.

We read of corporations encouraging meditation for stress reduction, yoga "breaks," and nutrition and exercise programs. The Adolph Coors Company has an extensive wellness program. "'The best way to control health-care costs is to prevent costs from occurring in the first place,' says Chairman William Coors, who himself meditates regularly. The field is still considered fringe medicine in some quarters—notably the insurance industry. But mind/body techniques are making inroads into the business world based largely on new credibility gained from recent scientific studies that suggest strong links between mental attitudes and physical health."[3]

3

Many of us enjoyed Bill Moyers' TV show on PBS in 1993, "Body, Mind, and Spirit," demonstrating that even national media are responding to the public recognition of a need for new understanding of the interrelationship of body, mind, and spirit. Mystics have always witnessed to a little-appreciated way of knowing. These forerunners are able to *comprehend* in a manner different from most of humanity.

*Nicholas Roerich (1874-1947), scholar, philosopher, humanitarian, world traveler, archaeologist, writer, and artist designed the Banner of Peace which he introduced to the world in 1929.

Figure 1. Banner of Peace. Three red disks encircled by a red ring on a field of white represent art, science, and religion. Through a synthesis of these three, Roerich believed, culture could unite humanity in peace.

An ignorant person must be civilized first of all, then educated, after which he becomes intelligent. Then comes refinement and realization of synthesis, which is crowned by the acceptance of the idea of culture . . . . Culture is synthesis. Culture knows and understands the foundations of life and creativeness, because it is the cult of worship or reverence for the creative fire, which is life.

—Nicholas Roerich

This is the evolutionary work divinely established in the mystery temples of the past. Those temples, more comparable to universities than to the churches of today, were to equip leaders to understand planetary life, its purpose, and its goal. These ideas filter down to us today in bits and pieces through the rituals and teachings of all religions and various esoteric and metaphysical traditions.

The Mental Mechanism

To begin our studies, we need to understand the building of the human mental mechanism, for it evolves in stages as humanity matures. The *three-brain concept makes fascinating reading.[4] Much more is going on than meets the eye as we do our day-to-day meditation practice. Often this is a missing piece of information for meditators. Figure 2 helps us comprehend the greater work in which we participate.

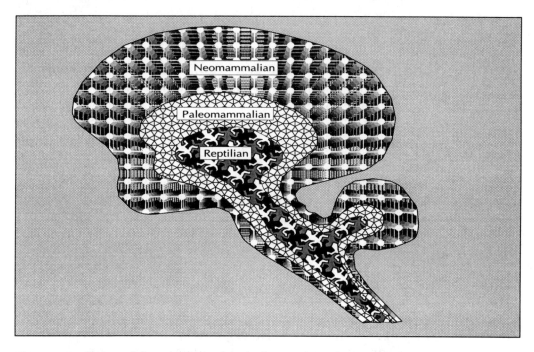

Figure 2. Evolution of the Human Brain. The human brain has evolved and expanded along the lines of three basic patterns, which may be characterized as reptilian, paleomammalian, and neomammalian (neocortex).

Old temple techniques emphasized strengthening and building a healthy body, performing practices in harmony with natural physical laws of evolution. Body maintenance is the work of the reptilian brain. Health and survival intelligence are anchored here, as is cellular development. This brain requires 1) repetition and 2) formality to establish the body's means of gathering intelligence.

From ancient times, meditation techniques have provided guidance in simple ways to fulfill these requirements. We utilize them to communicate with our body, to realize physical feats, or when working with the nature kingdoms.

Ancient and modern teachers suggest best results occur when we use the same place, same hour, and same style to meditate. A consistent opening and closing gesture (see page 20) is recommended. Repetitive chants and mantras help us alter consciousness. For centuries, monotonous prayers have been recited as a part of rituals, generally with few people understanding why. The use of mala beads and rosaries to address divinity has extended to modern times.

The next level of mind, the old mammalian or paleomammalian brain, calls for harmony, movement, and rhythm to develop. This brain level supports relationships. A sense of unity, nurturing, and feeling arises. Mammals relate instinctively to their own, be it cub or pack. Similarly, at this level of self, bonding and socialization occur. Ancient spiritual practices included swaying, dancing, marching, singing, and chanting because such rhythms and movement helped people align and achieve group identity.

Consider the stomp dance of our Native Americans, the hula dance of the Polynesians, monks walking as they sing Gregorian plainsong, and the chants and movements of the Eastern ashrams. These are but remnants of the ways we see this need fulfilled in a spiritual heritage we little understand.

> In the marvelous economy of nature, nothing is lost. Each progression life makes toward greater intelligence encompasses all previous gains. Our skulls, for instance, contain an old brain and a new brain. Our old brains are made of what is called the *reptilian brain* that is some 200 to 300 million years old (i.e., it was developed and perfected that long ago), and an *old mammalian brain* that is nearly as ancient. And it is through this system that we inherit the gains of the past.
> —Joseph Chilton Pearce, *Magical Child*

The Brain's Hemispheres

The "third brain"—the neocortex, or cerebral brain—refers to the left and right hemispheres and their unique functions. We relate to the whole of life with the right hemisphere. Integrative and sensitive, it is generally seen as the receiver of intuitive flashes. The left hemisphere serves to evaluate, analyze, and justify—especially designed to help us make choices in our everyday, outer life.

Each hemisphere is an important tool for living today:

- We catch a wonderful new idea, a flash—*right* hemisphere.
- We evaluate the idea—*left* hemisphere.
- We allow it to rest out of sight, pondering it from time to time, led by "what if" imaging—*right* hemisphere.
- We list steps it will require to activate the idea—*left* hemisphere.
- As we develop the idea on the material plane, we improve it creatively—*right.*
- We gather resources—*left*—until the project is completed.

The neocortex requires 1) stimulation and 2) curiosity to utilize its resources. Inventors (such as Thomas Edison), creative thinkers (Frank Lloyd Wright), and noted artists (Walt Disney) especially embodied the powerful capabilities of the neocortex to guide humanity into the future.

Our rational intellectualism is the province of the left hemisphere with its talent for evaluating, rationalizing, and judging. It was designed to assist us with our individualism, and we have used it well.

Passive meditation utilizes right hemisphere capabilities when we are guided to envision places, colors, smells—all the psychic mechanisms—and are taken to a state of openness to guidance. Known techniques for stimulating the spiritual senses and magnifying our desire for information, guidance, or inner contact are designed to fulfill the requirements of this level of brain so we may connect with all our capabilities. In this openness, a flash of knowing or insight may be experienced.

> *Do not neglect the gifts that you have. . . . Meditate upon these things; give yourself wholly to them, so that it may be known to all that you are progressing.*
>
> 1 Timothy 4.14,15

With its use of imagination and drama, passive meditation comes down to us from past ages, perhaps even from Atlantean times. Temples used tapestries, paintings, and mystery plays to stimulate the inner senses and to develop imagination. Such tools link the seeker to archetypes held in the *collective unconscious and stimulate the hidden potential. Little aware of other levels of intelligence at work deep within us, we see the well-developed neocortex as most important today. Every high civilization trained those who demonstrated aspiration and discipline to provide leadership for the people. Moreover, the untrained did not realize how the powerful mind of collective humanity shaped planetary events.

Today, as we emerge from the *kali-yuga—a period of ignorance, destruction, and planetary blight which has engulfed humanity for some time—we are rapidly regaining seemingly lost knowledge. The part we each play in the condition of humankind and in the evolution of planetary life is being recalled. Although difficult to comprehend for some, others seem to respond instinctively to this concept.

We need to understand two great truths: 1) humanity collectively forms the mental mechanism for planetary life, and 2) we can either live on the planet from a lower personality level with its continuing struggle or we can assist collectively to lift human life to a wiser level. A spiritualized level of understanding will provide insights to a great Plan of which humanity is but a part. Wise ones will lead us to a restored Garden of Eden where peace and harmony await. Ancient teachings assure us humanity will rediscover high consciousness and again, as we read in Genesis, 3.8, *walk and talk with God.*

This intent is held by many spiritually aware ones who believe themselves to be part of the interface between inner and outer realities. Meditation is the principal bridge between the worlds, as they are commonly called. We might also say, spirit and matter.

> He who is a giant may take giant steps but for ordinary man, build him a ladder or stairway.
>
> —Bill King, Ph.D.[5]

A New Brain

We are told an additional level of brain mechanism is under development within the evolving human. The next brain, the prefrontal lobe, has been called the "Buddha bump." The futuristic head is described as elongated with a higher brow; senses will be more refined and mental perception particularly sharpened. This next-stage brain development offers humanity new abilities: conscious awareness, or *continuity of consciousness, and other skills of the adept. The important factor is that our latent soul powers are to become conscious. Contacts or veiled connections with guidance will occur more readily in the more awakened state. Naturally telepathic practitioners will be more open to the heavenly inhabitants and to powers of mind not yet realized.

I suggest we think of Wise Ones, or so-called "Masters," and their advanced capabilities as the divinely designed human of the future. The next kingdom, the kingdom of souls, will be such as they. John 14.12 will be fulfilled: *He who believes in me shall do the works which I do; and even greater than these things he shall do.* The glorious potential of humanity inspires us to strive to become this new being modeled in the lives of the holy ones.

	Reptilian	Paleomammalian	Neomammalian or Neocortex	Prefrontal Lobe
Purpose:	Health and communication between systems of the body	Relationship of parts to the whole	Rational process Analytical ability Evaluation Judgment	Kingdom of Souls to manifest
Development Needs:				
	Repetition Formality Chants	Rhythm Movement Sing-song Feelings	Curiosity Newness Questioning Exploration	Focus on abstractions Expansion of consciousness

Figure 3. Conscious Recapitulation of Brain Development.

We have limitless possibilities to find fulfillment and satisfaction in our lives and in our relationships with one another. By learning to directly contact the essence of our being, we can discover an unbounded freedom which is not only a freedom *from* some external restraint, but is itself the dynamic expression

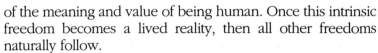

of the meaning and value of being human. Once this intrinsic freedom becomes a lived reality, then all other freedoms naturally follow.

—Tarthang Tulku, *Time, Space, and Knowledge*[6]

Techniques provided to aspirants always begin with the needs of the reptilian brain, as we do in this course work: formality and repetition (posture and chanting), relaxing and centering again and again.

Gradually the techniques of mammalian brain are integrated: movement, chanting, mantras, dance, and expression of worship, stimulating the heart without intellectualism. The imagination is at last engaged. The mind screen is built, and astral cleansing begins. Here we see the value of guided meditation set into motion. Symbolic journeys and archetypes stir and awaken—blessing—and do battle as needed.

Now comes the next step, the grasping of a variety of realities through the neocortex. The tools to be used here are curiosity, stimulation, and newness. We learn to work "as if," to question inwardly, to find the awareness that correlates the activity of the right and left hemispheres. Heart and mind are stirred, for both are needed for right relationship in the outer world.

As we continue, passive meditation helps us bond with our higher self and our basic self; we unearth our vulnerable areas and effect healing. We discover our strengths as well, and receive encouragement. After attention to this level of our inner life, we are ready for seed-thought work and for the realization of ourselves as taught in the "I Am the Soul" methodology.

The *dharma light—the lawgiver, the source—responds through the silence from what seems empty, unmoving, and quiet, with sound, color, richness, and all-knowing. The mystic hears and sees and knows, yet only within the self can the way be found. No frantic effort or loud demand will open this door. It is to be found behind the silence, the mystic silence of inner quiet.

At the highest point of this celestial structure . . . one finds Dharma, Cosmic Law, all the principles of right action . . . Dharma is the silent order that upholds all activity in the universe. It regulates the motions of the galaxies and planets, the seasons, and all the activities of nature. It is also the power that upholds all correct behavior in the human sphere and discourages all activity that is wrong. The vision of this structure is of the greatest practical value, for it reveals the still center from which all harmonious action emerges. In India, those saints who are in accord with this silent hub of Dharma are thought to emit a spiritual power that, though unseen, exerts an orderly influence on the environment, freeing it from all kinds of misfortune. Thus the activity of *seeing* this inner axis of the universe was thought to be more important than a million good deeds, for the *seeing* would prevent harmful activities from occurring for miles around. This is why in the East skillful inaction is considered to be a tremendously potent form of action.

—James N. Powell
The Tao of Symbols[7]

Somehow we must come to know the importance of inner silence and the thoughts that waft here. We delight in each discovery; every response fills our heart with warmth, yet we blush to tell another of our mystery. We want to run and share, to tell another, but as we speak the words, how foolish we feel, for we know it is ours only. Golden tones fall flat as we speak them now. They are only ours.

We must learn to trust, holding each thought tight until tried. We use each drop of wisdom to build trust and courage. The trust renews the inner ear, the courage prepares us for the work ahead. The steps are aligned in such a way as to take the strength of the using to help free us from pain. We strengthen our readiness through discrimination and response to each insight. Some are for the self alone, some for sharing, some for knowing, and some must wait until the right season arrives. Our eager human nature grasps the sacred sense of timing, and so the challenges break forth from our own inner ear to our world. We sow the seed and reap the harvest. Now we know, and again we bend to the silence that whispers.

Sacred signs lead to the mystery of the Greater, though many vanish in the harshness of the outer mind. We come to know, and we come to be. Patience comes with wisdom to the waiting one.

Introducing Agni Yoga

Both Nicholas and *Helena Roerich (1879-1949), who received the Agni Yoga teachings, encouraged the idea of working through our ignorance with a spiritual guide. They saw this mentor existing in a variety of forms: as a sage with a liberated soul, as an avatar or deity, or as a spiritual aspirant's High Self. The spiritual journey is the liberating experience of learning to hear and to follow the voice of the inner guru.

The Roerichs were Russian Orthodox Christians ahead of their time. Helena was a woman of intellect and education who joined her husband in an appreciation of culture. A visitation by *Master Morya led to her lifetime purpose serving as his amanuensis for the dictation of the Agni Yoga teachings. These writings provide a contemporary path with instructions that serve well both those who practice a particular religion and those who do not. Their inclusiveness helps practitioners become people of equality, ecumenical and international in nature. The Roerichs' reverence for the Christ and respect for the hierarchy of holy ones prompts us to include contributions from Agni Yoga in these meditation lessons.

Compatible with holy thought of both East and West and practical for those of all religious persuasions—or none—Agni Yoga teachings especially appeal to those who seek that point of consciousness wherein we all become One.

Agni Yoga—or "ethical living," as these writings are often called—suggests that fervor and purification of the physical, emotional, and mental bodies will bring transformation to our everyday lives. This path advocates the practice of meditation to connect our inner and outer lives, and the clearing of glamours and illusions. It is believed the formation and application of a living ethic will engender the development of virtues within the personality and characterize the modern spiritual life-styling associated by many with the birth of a new era in human history.

The journey to enlightenment begins by dialoguing with companions of the outer world, learning to select wise friends, spiritually questing with friends and foes alike, and, in time, with a wise and sharing teacher or disciple. The truth made clear within the self draws us to the inner teacher or guru. The once foolish who found all pleasure in the adventures of the outer may now delight in solitude or in simple pleasures with the like-minded.

The spiritual search unfolds in a known pattern. The outer is not enough. The like-minded delight in one another, but in time, mere spiritual companionship is no longer adequate; that which is of greatest value must be humbly placed into the Holy Hand. Now the ascending step must be taken, and the realization dawns that a misty door has opened to carry the dedicated one out of sight. From now on, only partially can this be grasped; too much inner has occurred for the outer world to restrain this seeker. Gradually we clear away the clutter and find ourselves in a gentle place. Now we begin to touch into that which waits in the silence.

Preparation for the Inner Journey

Attitudes

As we ready ourselves for this intimate journey, we start with fundamentals. Our attitude toward meditation is vital. We must eliminate thoughts of success and failure and allow a variation from day to day in what we experience and feel. Ideas that emerge, understandings we develop, emotional and even mystical experiences we have, our sensory responses—all are incidental phenomena. Their occurrence, or lack of occurrence, is not as important as engaging in the continuing process. Our experiences fluctuate in intensity according to how we feel, our physical energy level, and the demands on our time. "Doing" is all the success we need. I often say, "Just put yourself in posture." Whatever we do is what we can experience at the time, and that is enough.

A great hindrance to the practice of meditation is that we must dedicate valuable time to doing it. A second challenge is that it looks as though we are not doing anything. We think of our chores and falsely believe we cannot "just sit there." So now we must dedicate some time to the process, and we must believe we are, in fact, doing something. It is real; it is just out of sight. Doing our practice consistently depends upon our knowing it has value and it is accomplishing something.

The Purpose of Silence

As we begin to think with the higher part of our nature, we establish a dialogue with the "word" that dwells within. We watch as this communication becomes clearer with regular experiences of silence.

When we first begin to hold ourselves in the silence, it seems strange. We think of silence as lack of outer noise. Then it becomes an inner focus interrupted by remembering tasks to be done, thoughts about the outer life in which we are engaged, troubles or relationships that need attention—each demanding that some of this newly found space be focused upon it. We do so briefly, making a list or fulfilling the forgotten task. Gradually we clear away the clutter of this inner space, and we find ourselves in a calm, gentle place. Now we connect to the next level of silence.

This next silence brings us rest, peace, and healing for irritated nerves. It is at first a balm; then impulses of new thought rise to the mind's surface. This gentle movement is such that, if we resist, it stops. Its subtle presence either gains a gentle hold on us or it evades our conscious notice and becomes lost in the relaxed state as a pleasantness.

Should we dialogue mentally with the authoritative word that seeks to be in touch with us, we discover another depth of inner self. We find ideas usually attributed to creativity surging upward for review or thoughts breaking through with a rush that we would call "fire" or "enthusiasm," new ideas to act upon. A realization surfaces with a long-awaited answer. The thoughts this inner presence releases seem to float as magnets into the universal mind, drawing information and responses back, and with deeper perception.

This intense kind of inner dialogue, whether called conversation with a higher power or talking with God, is usually best approached through some ritualistic entry of our own unique style. Rarely can we give the key to another, but we who discover the doorway come to know that we start with a particular ritual, unconsciously, to carry us into this "right feeling" so the process may begin. I hesitate to say it is prayer, for that suggests outer concepts; this is more a dialogue with self, a seeking. We come to ask, and in the asking, the door opens and response comes.

Esoteric teachings encourage us to develop a relationship to both God-Transcendent and God-Immanent. As children, most of us were introduced to concepts of God "out there" and prayer as either worship or communication with the Creator. Few of us receive an early introduction to God-Immanent, the spark of God within us. While this inner divinity is ever present, communication with it may be the progressive next step in our personal spirituality; it has been for many. Meditation is the principle means of communication, although dreams, impressions, body awareness, and intuition assist in the process. Various names have been given this *Inner Presence, but most common are the Transpersonal Self, the Self, the Christ-Within, the Atman, the Divine Presence, and the High Self. (In this course we will incline toward universal language.)

As we begin to think with the higher part of our nature, we establish a dialogue with the "word" that dwells within. We watch as this communication becomes clearer from regular experiences with silence.

We are respectfully approaching a law of the universe. We know we are as children crying out for the wisdom of the Greater. We may be humble or haughty, but the intensity builds until the breakthrough; let us say, the creativity ignites within us, and the holy drama of God and human engenders interaction.

Disciplined creativity following a certain respectful manner gains entry, and the Great Creator bends a holy ear to hear; the dialogue begins and wisdom flows. All mystics know this contact, this happening, this response. Whether the happening is "God said" or "I received," the realness validates, and the heart is filled. This holy word persists through the experiences of life, and belief and sureness become the reward. We come to say, "I know how it is for me." We become attuned to the inner self in such a way that one ear listens inwardly to the silence, and the other listens to the world.

To build our receptive mechanism, we commit to putting ourselves in posture time and time again. We take a receptive position and merely "be with" our procedure. Acquiescence is absolutely necessary, a conscious consent to allow something abstract, vague, and indefinable to occur. Granting ourselves permission allows the subtle part of self, usually kept under wraps by the critic part, the analytical evaluator of all we do, to emerge. Just assuming a posture of being with the inner self without demands can change our lives. Holding no expectations and no immediate requirements is quite different from our usual approach to life. That difference requires we adapt. Thus, we take step one.

We must remember, our meditation experiences are uniquely our own. Whatever they may be, they are neither better nor worse than those of another. Any need to compete is inappropriate. While sometimes we may feel competitive or envious or wish for another's experiences, we will learn to recognize this as the programming of our highly competitive society, and we release any feeling of guilt associated with our desire. We know the inner presence will make itself known in its own time and way. We must simply be willing to put ourselves in posture time and time again and accept whatever happens or doesn't happen. *The commitment is to put ourselves in posture.* Just think, "If God wants to find me, I'll be listening." Don't make it hard; just be there:

Wait on the Lord: be of good courage and he shall strengthen thine heart: wait, I say, on the Lord.

Psalm 27.14

Focusing primarily upon spiritual development tends to keep attitudes and responses on a constructive, centered path. Remember, each of us is a channel through which life is already flowing. We use a spiritual focus—prayer or devotional reading—prior to each meditation session to help us center on noble ideas before beginning.

Do not be anxious about the suggested procedures. Suitable preparation, reasonable regularity, comfort, and freedom from distraction allow us to concentrate on the essence of meditation. But they are not rigid requirements, just suggested aids.

When you first decide to meditate, be prepared for resistance from the physical body. It has become used to the conscious mind constantly trying to fulfill its needs; now we want to still the mind and relax the body. Neither chooses to be quieted. Every part will itch, hurt, or need to wiggle. We must handle the body gently and patiently, as though dealing with a young child. You may even choose to direct a few words or thoughts to the body to help it adjust. If you are accustomed to sitting quietly, the body usually will have less difficulty. For most of us it is the mind that revolts and will not be still. Then we have to give it something to do while we get on with opening the inner door.

Physical Setting, Relaxation, and Centering

To begin, establish a time and place free from distraction. This does not mean perfectly quiet, but the telephone should be disconnected or at least in another room. Sudden, loud noises will be startling. Just as a regular study time and place are good for us when we are attending school, most meditators find it advantageous to use the same place at about the same time each day. Early morning, before eating or starting the routine of the day, is a preferred time, but it may not be practical in all living situations. For years, with my many children, early morning was not possible, so 11 p.m. was my time. While regularity helps to integrate these new experiences more comfortably, you must do what works for you. But do remember the value of practice. If you currently meditate once weekly, try two times a week. Any increase is progress.

Most of us experiment a little to determine that just-right position. The early Egyptians used to sit very upright on a chair with eyes straight ahead, palms down on the knees, heels together, feet flat. Many people today sit much the same way, with their eyes closed. Eastern Indians mostly meditate sitting cross-legged upon the ground in what we call the "lotus" posture. The Chinese squat or use various postures difficult for most of us to maintain.

In the process of training our subconscious mind to be still and obedient, after a little practice, whenever we go to our meditation chair or our meditation spot, our physical nature begins to adjust. Meditation teachers generally suggest twenty minutes at a session.

However, you may find that sometimes your meditation happens more quickly and easily, and you are just as satisfied.

As possible, find an area to call your own, and dedicate it to your spiritual work. Be comfortable enough to sit for fifteen to thirty minutes. It may be in a chair, on a bench, or in the lotus position. A sitting position with the back erect is usually best for Westerners.

Become comfortable with investing time and effort in the centering technique. If you sit in a chair, learn to sit straight rather than leaning back. Good posture is basic for deep relaxation. Slide forward so your back does not touch the chair, allowing your body to become an antenna, vibrant with energy. We want to tune the physical vehicle to be receptive to the energy we contact. This is a gradual process—allow it to happen. Learn to relax with the body erect, feel the altered state begin, and then hold yourself upright, off the back of the chair. If you tire, slump and rest briefly, then straighten again.

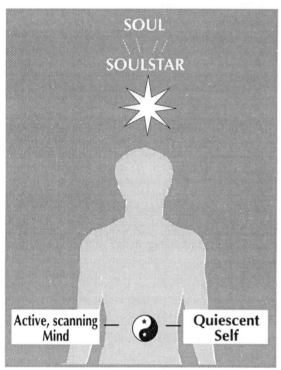

Figure 4. Quiescent Self: The Home of the Human Seed.

If we lie down to meditate, we tend to go to sleep. If not seated properly in a chair, we may slump and cause distracting muscle tensions. When we are seated comfortably, we begin with relaxation and centering procedures. While these may seem fairly elaborate in early lessons, later, or when we more easily become quiet and centered, relaxation can be achieved quickly and simply. It is important to prepare physically and mentally so more attention can be given to the meditation process. These are the basics; later lessons contain more advanced procedures. The techniques we offer are progressive, allowing time and practice to prepare you for each new stage.

In a complete explanation of why centering is so important, there should be included the introduction of the *quiescent self, a term relatively unknown. Let's look at it in this way, though this explanation is somewhat simplified. The soul puts down a *soulstar, a point of light over the head. A personality through which we experience is projected from this point. Our experiences build the High Self's *ball of knowledge, and we will call upon this ball of knowledge when it is needed.

The subtle quiescent self, or quiet self, contains a stepped-down connection to the soulstar. We are more familiar with the active, scanning mind that protects ego, always involved with survival and self-indulgence, i.e., gratifying its own needs. When we are learning to become centered and balanced, we calm this scanning, restless survival mind and become aware of a soft, quiet point of light that provides a feeling of well-being. This point of light needs to be magnified to balance with our survival instinct, the programming we have received, and the left-hemisphere mind power gathered over a lifetime. Learning to be centered then involves calming the active side of the self and becoming increasingly sensitive to the subtle self, whom we may never have met before.

This quiescent self waits. Passive in nature until invoked, it represents the High Self at its most basic level. This is the seat of the psychic nature and ultimately reveals itself as clairsentience. Right now our work is to calm the ego mind. Repeated calming work teaches ego that it is safe to rest, to trust, to learn, or, as we hear so often today, to "go with the flow."

Numerology is the only major spiritual science that has kept the term "quiescent self" so we may easily see the imprint this generic human seed carries. It provides the best clues to the nature of the hidden or quiet self, and it has something to offer today's seekers.

In esoteric thought:

Numbers are representative of forces which operate on the highest spiritual planes . . . Every number possesses an individual keynote, and, as we gain comprehension of the spiritual meaning of these several keynotes, we discover new and deeper meanings . . . with which they are in attunement.
—Corinne Heline, *Sacred Science of Numbers*[8]

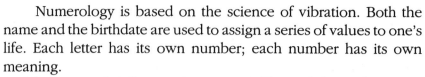

Numerology is based on the science of vibration. Both the name and the birthdate are used to assign a series of values to one's life. Each letter has its own number; each number has its own meaning.

The three main influences in a person's life are 1) the Soul Urge (the vowels), 2) the Expression (the consonants), and 3) the Life Path (the total of vowels and consonants). The Soul Urge is the number of your heart's desire, that which you would like most to do. The Expression is the sum of your natural capacities and capabilities, your talents and possibilities. The Life Path is the *where* of your life, your opportunities.

By calculation and study, an individual gains insight into traits, strengths and weaknesses, as well as an assigned theme for life. Personal years and universal years are also often studied to enrich an awareness of one's purpose and pattern. Each number has a significance and numerologists use basic formulas to discover helpful impressions regarding the participant.

Your latent or quiescent self is your *consonant* sum. This number is quiescent because not active in your daily life. Your vowels are always active in your soul; your vowels and consonants together are active in your Expression; your consonants are active only in the individual letters, but their sum is you *at rest*. Your consonant number is your own secret for it is *you* devoid of the necessity for aspiration or ambition, *you* when you are alone, concerned only with your own dreams, relieved from responding to outside influences. As soon as another person or idea enters your atmosphere you have a reaction, and are no longer quiescent or wholly *consonantal.*

—Florence Campbell
Your Days Are Numbered[9]

The quiescent self is the hidden human seed that will in time express its gift through the integrated personality. Right now, it awaits its opportunity.

Opening and Closing Gestures

Prior to beginning meditation, select your opening and closing gesture. In early Christian rituals the sign of the cross was adopted. In many traditions celebrants bow their heads with palms placed together. Some touch their chest above the heart.

Hands placed in the characteristic prayer position with palms together and making a slight bow is loved by many, especially as a closing gesture. Moving both hands, palms together, from the brow center to slightly over the head (crown *chakra) and back down to rest at the heart helps me remember I am centering myself and invoking inspiration from the Higher, so I prefer this for an opening gesture.

It does not matter what the gesture is, but it is important that we select one and become consistent in our use of it. By signaling the basic self and facilitating contact with the reptilian brain, we are teaching body, emotions, and mind to work together. This gesture provides repetition and formality. Custom adds stability to our practice and gains the cooperation of the basic self. We adopt the same gesture for opening and closing our various meditations.

The question has been asked, "What if the meditator cannot visualize the soulstar over his/her head?" Try the following procedure as a way to capture at a sensory level the experience of the light. Sit directly under a floor lamp close enough to feel the heat of the lamp on the top of your head. Feel the heat on your body, open your eyes, and see the shower of light surrounding you. Now sit for a few minutes and imprint the experience in your mind. Know that from now on you can reconstruct the feelings of this experience from memory. Upon command, you can reconstruct the light over your head or the light flowing around you. It is quite likely this awareness of the soul practiced regularly will lead to even richer experiences.

Basic steps have to precede the ability to really meditate. Let us look at and practice these first two exercises. Evaluate yourself, please, as you proceed.

EXERCISE—LEARNING RELAXATION

1st Step: We have to learn to sit quietly and allow the body to relax. Usually closing our eyes hastens the process, so we do that. When the body is truly relaxed, natural healing energies move through it, restoring balance and, thus, health.

Whether or not we truly seek to *know* in any kind of inner way, we may choose to reduce stress and enjoy improved health by learning some kind of deep relaxation.

A few nice slow breaths will help. Breathe in slowly, hold for just a few seconds. Breathe out—nice, long, and slow. Repeat five or six times.

My suggestion is to call this a first step to develop a relaxation technique. Repeat ten minutes twice a day for a week or so, or as needed, before you proceed to truly practice meditation.

If you are doing some kind of meditation and feel your body is already relaxing well, proceed to Step 2.

2nd Step: Test for relaxation. Focus now on your emotional state, and particularly note if you are holding tension at the solar plexus level. If so, breathe in and out deeply three or four more times in long slow breaths. Observe your body through your inner perception, with eyes closed. Wherever you notice tension, focus briefly on that part of the body with the thought, "Relax, let go," drawing in new energy to the tense area and allowing it to become comfortable.

Now, aware that your solar plexus is relaxed, peaceful, and ready to create confidence and strength, envision a light at the solar plexus surrounded by an aura of calm. Feel yourself peaceful, secure, and self-assured. The solar plexus is the home of lower mind, ruler of personality life, which is now able to assist in the alignment of personality and quiescent self.

Let us move our attention to the heart center. Dwell on your heart and sense a light surrounding it as you think to yourself, "I care, I care."

Allow yourself to become deeply aware of the Great Life of which we are each but a part. Now experience a sense of love. Be at peace in the love that flows.

Perhaps this seems to you merely a step in an exercise to get to true meditation. Do not think of it that way. The ultimate breakthrough in meditation work depends on your undertaking each step fully so that you will be prepared for the next. Involving your emotional level and allowing yourself to rest in the Great Love is a way to connect to the astral battery, empowering yourself to do more.

So, let us focus on the work that is a part of the emotional nature. Think, "I care," repeatedly, and truly let yourself be lost in the process of caring. Go to the place where you feel vulnerable. When you begin to feel fearful of stretching any further, settle yourself, and focus on becoming stable, comfortable, and "caring."

Say to yourself: "I would care about all of life. I dare to love life seen and unseen, known and unknown. I care, I care." Feel this growing love energy at work within you.

Next, and from time to time, say quietly:

I forgive the experiences that have brought me pain. I forgive myself and I forgive others. I release the bruises and hurts, and I retain the new awareness gathered from each experience. I release the limitation of the past and dare to be radiant with new energy of the soul.

Allow the sense of soul energy, love in the truest sense—**L**ots **O**f **V**ital **E**nergy—to flow into the personality, clearing and cleansing, that personality might be molded to the purposes of the soul.

As this inflow of energy blesses the personality, it reaches every level of our nature. The body is touched by the energy—healing, aligning, and centering. We bless the body, directing healing energy to wherever there is need. Allow the love you have contacted to permeate your body. See it as light moving from cell to cell, from organ to organ, and system to system. Bless your body, and thank it for the service it has given. Continue in this way for a few moments until you perceive your body ready to allow that light to emanate into the aura about you. Continue your day in this positive field of energy.

Imagine your aura like an eggshell—transparent, encompassing—filling with the energy you have contacted in your loving heart. Bring this positive radiant energy to swirl about you—over the head, behind the knees, beneath the feet—clearing and cleansing your personal space of all negativity, old thoughtforms, or attitudes that you no longer need.

Now imagine the aura field around you emanating to others the energy you have drawn earthward. See positive energy flowing through you into the room, the environment, the world. Breathe. Relax. Rest.

Be gentle with yourself. Take a nice long breath as you prepare to return to the world about you. Close the aura, and fill the area about you with bright light as you gently draw your attention outward, retaining an awareness of inward well-being and an outer shield of positive energy. Adopt and use a closing gesture. For now I suggest bringing your palms together, a slight bow of respect to the higher world, and a closing word: *Shanti, Shalom, Amen,* or another of your choice. Now, bring your attention outward.

In these lessons you are reminded to begin by *just doing the work;* as lessons proceed, you will be guided in how to improve techniques and move from level to level. The first step is always to *begin.* Refinement comes with established practice. You practice, please, and we will suggest ideas to refine the procedure. Without practice, many additional ideas have no gift to offer.

Results When Centered	
Physical Body	Relaxation occurs Healing energy flows Revitalization increases Stress decreases
Emotional Nature	New love (Lots Of Vital Energy) flows Positive energy is experienced Good will emanates
Mental Level	Peace of mind is realized A new clarity emerges as witness consciousness is built Serenity spontaneously occurs
Spiritual Life	Creativity stirs Inspiration flashes New realizations are conceived

Figure 5. The Attributes of Each Level When Centered.

AN EXERCISE IN CENTERING

Light a candle and invoke higher light. Cleanse the room with incense and become comfortable. Release body tensions by gradually breathing a few deep breaths. Give the body a mental command to relax, become centered, and be at peace. Allow natural healing energy to flow freely through each level of your being. Enjoy a sense of centeredness and harmony.

Become aware of the bright light of your soulstar shining upon you from over your head. Bring your attention to the solar plexus, drawing down the light from over your head to expand the field of light at your power center. Illumined with light, the rational mind becomes more peaceful, at rest, and relaxed. Say to yourself: "There is one power in the universe, and it blesses me." Relax, and repeat once again, "There is one power in the universe, and it blesses me." Pay attention to the breath, stay relaxed, and allow yourself to settle more deeply into the peace of the moment. Allow this peace of mind to grant you freedom from all concerns. Be free to be.

Now focus on the heart, creating a sensation of "awesome-ness," a sense of love, gratitude, and appreciation for life itself—all of life, the pleasant and the challenging. Breathe in slowly, rhythmically; then breathe out, holding the awe in your heart and allowing life to just be. Care for, love, and be with the energy of life in a gentle, restful way—one with it all, no limitations. All barriers dissolve. Breathe in, and think, "allow." Breathe out. Rest in the sea of universal energy.

Again now, take an in-breath, and move your attention to the head. Fill it with light, over, within, and about the head, charging yourself with a radiance that reflects the soulstar. Permeated with the light, the mind radiates through and around the physical body, forming the halo of light familiar to us all. Think, "I am the soul." Repeat this peaceful mantra over and over, "I am the soul," and sense the inner connection of solar plexus, heart, and mind.

For about five minutes, stay in this relaxed and focused awareness of your true nature: *soul experiencing life in the physical.* Continue to breathe gently in long, rhythmic, slow breaths—inhale, exhale—centered in the great peace known to the wise. When you have finished, before moving your attention outward, speak a

*power word aloud three times, as a soul-infused being: **Om, *Shalom, *Shanti,* or another with which you are comfortable. Then in a gentle and easy fashion, return your awareness to the body. Move gently, stretch a bit. Feeling refreshed by your inner contact, celebrate the joy of high consciousness. Now open your eyes, renewed.

Meditation Approaches
Past, Present, and Future

But we all, with open faces,
see as in a mirror the glory of the Lord,
and we shall be transformed into the same likeness,
from one glory to another,
just as the Spirit comes from the Lord.

2 Corinthians 3.18

We transit from one point in consciousness to another as we grow. We reach a pleasant plateau, internalize our oasis, become familiar with the terrain, and learn to defend it. However, when we grow, we become uncomfortable, forced to look again at our old processes, practices, and habits. We see what part of yesterday's rationale is still applicable and what must be remodeled. Moving along in life and in consciousness is taxing. It makes us weary. We tire of having to redo and often reach a point where we want to stop striving and just crystallize. This is the very crux of the human problem.

Within each of us, one part wants to grow and another wants to stop and rest. Those who fail to meet this challenge do not necessarily go astray; they may simply rest too long. Then deterioration sets in, just as unused muscles soften and atrophy. Spiritual challenge keeps discrimination active, but it may evaporate if we become sluggish and believe we have found "the way."

Consciousness brings more pain, but it also brings more joy. Because as you go further into the desert—if you go far enough—you will begin to discover little patches of green, little oases that you had never seen before. And if you go still further, you may even discover some streams of living water underneath the sand, or if you go still further, you may even be able to fulfill your own ultimate destiny.

—M. Scott Peck
Further Along the Road Less Traveled

With this insight we begin to see there is nothing new to be said but to change the image-making receiver set and listen again to the old words with new ears. It is neither new nor old to substitute metaphysical words. It is the same "going to God," attuning to meaningful techniques. Age-old and age-new, it is all in the eyes and ears of the beholder. As we seek high consciousness, we are not the first adventurers or even the first exciting "new agers" of the group mind; we are only the current ones.

Centuries ago, the Benedictine tradition offered the discipline of *lectio divina,* "sacred reading," a four-part process involving *lectio,* reading; *oratorio,* personal prayer; *meditatio,* meditation; and *contemplatio,* contemplation.

The reasoning behind this practice is simple but potent, as revolutionary as the yeast buried in three measures of flour by the woman in the Gospel (Matthew 13.33). If we devote a few minutes each day attuning to God's word, we can change. Note the word "can."

"As you are, so is the world," says Ramana Maharishi. As we change, so does the world. Nothing dramatic is needed, just the daily smoothing of the sharp edges of selfishness and ego. Then an attitude forms within us that permeates our reality, so we may strive to live this high consciousness all the day.

Meditation is designed to bring us closer to the Source of All Reality, to interface human mind with Divine Mind. In the beginning, we may comprehend little of what happens intellectually, but we can experience and find explanations later. Awe-inspiring wisdom remains lightly veiled until we are ready. After years of personal practice, we find ourselves continuing to be enriched, uplifted, and blessed by spiritual experiences.

Some people meditate for years, yet seem not to progress very far toward understanding and freedom. Certainly it is not a cure-all, but a regular practice does set into motion the process of change. Those who meditate to reduce stress may discontinue it as they feel better. Others become so involved with the dynamics and dramatics of the process, they seem to lose their way. Still others realize vast life changes distinctly related to their meditation practice. Apparently, then, both how and why we practice meditation influence the outcome considerably.

These lessons are designed to develop spirituality as a foundation for living in the here and now, which is best accomplished by a regular meditation practice that expands awareness. Meditation may be new to you, or you may have tried forms of it in the past with unimpressive or disappointing results. Due to the range of experience of our readers, we provide a wide spectrum of content so as to bring an enriched level of understanding to all students.

Meditation—the Doorway Behind Which the Soul Awaits

Almost all books on yoga, spiritual development, esoteric and religious ideas, or psychological self-help include some discussion of meditation. Books devoted to meditation would fill a sizable bookcase, and sampling the many techniques could become quite confusing. It seems the authors are not even writing about the same thing. Some procedures promise immediate benefits, while others talk in terms of a lifetime of dedicated effort. The process may be described as frustratingly difficult or surprisingly simple, an effortless effort. Meditation may be seen as a way of resolving daily problems and conflicts or as an experience far surpassing problem-solving.

The greater goal of this course is to facilitate soul infusion. This concept prepares the personality for alignment with the soul to produce an awareness of the purpose for which we have incarnated. Stages of maturity lead us from "unaware of" and "separated from" this inner nature to, in time, an integrated personality, all aspects of personality working well together. No longer are heart

Spirituality

The New Age is characterized by spirituality. In essence, spirituality is simply living with intention to realize God in every circumstance of your being—thoughts, emotions, words, deeds, relations, aspirations—in short, the totality of your life, right through its very end (as saints and sages do by "dying the good death"). As I have said before: That attitude, that stance in life is the only thing which can truly create a better world. There will never be a better world until there are better people in it. The way to build better people is to begin with yourself by realizing God. To realize God means to know God on every level of reality and in every mode or aspect of God's being. Thus, spirituality can be defined, level by level of reality, this way:

In *physical* terms, spirituality is recognizing the miraculous nature of matter and the creative source behind the mystery of matter.

In *biological* terms, spirituality is realizing that a divine intelligence underlies all life-change and that such change is evolving all creation to ever greater degrees of wholeness in order to perfectly express itself.

In *psychological* terms, spirituality is discovering within yourself the ultimate source of meaning and happiness, which is love.

In *sociological* terms, spirituality is giving selfless service to others, regardless of race, creed, color, gender, caste, or nationality.

In *ecological* terms, spirituality is showing respect for all the kingdoms in the community of life—mineral, vegetable, animal, human, spirit, and angelic.

In *cosmological* terms, spirituality is being at one with the universe, in tune with the infinite, flowing with the Tao.

In *theological* terms, spirituality is seeing God in all things, all events, and all circumstances, indwelling as infinite light and unconditional love, and seeing all things, events, and circumstances in God as the matrix or infinite ocean in which the universe occurs.

—John White, *The Meeting of Science and Spirit*[1]

and mind engaged in battle, nor are body instincts resisting harmony with the whole. Integrated personality is ready for a next stage of experience, a purpose. Soul infusion results as personality adapts to accommodate soul and responds to its impulses.

For every incarnated soul there exists a learning, a purpose, a goal. We are both spirit and matter; meditation unlocks the doorway between the two realities, the doorway through which we perceive, intuit, and know. As awareness expands, we come to realize our reason for being in this incarnation.

Many authorities classify types of meditation by describing differences in techniques or procedures. Ram Dass[2] describes nine activities which represent forms of meditation. Haridas Chaudhuri,[3] under methods of meditation, presents twelve different activities; some are whole systems of procedures. Others have tried to note common elements in various activities in order to classify the forms. Richard Hittleman[4] distinguishes active from passive meditation. To him, active includes body, mind, and experiential activities with a focus on increased awareness of the world and our participation in it. Passive forms incorporate deep relaxation, concentration, and directing the life force, both with and without "seed." Meditation "with seed" involves some degree of mental focus on an idea or concept to derive the essence behind or beyond the "seed."

> Solitary reading will enable a man to stuff himself with information, but without conversation, his mind will become like a pond without an outlet—a mass of unhealthy stagnature (stagnation). It is not enough to harvest knowledge by study; the wind of talk must winnow it and blow away the chaff. Then will the clear, bright grains of wisdom be garnered, for our own use or that of others.
>
> —William Matthews[5]

In this course the terms "passive" and "active" refer to differences in the mental state during meditation. The passive approach involves a relaxed openness, with a gentle expansion toward complete peace and sense of being, without much effort or using those techniques which require following a guide. The active approach focuses energies for a breakthrough of understanding and knowing. Other techniques include purification; healing; and

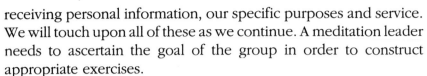

receiving personal information, our specific purposes and service. We will touch upon all of these as we continue. A meditation leader needs to ascertain the goal of the group in order to construct appropriate exercises.

While passive techniques[6] provide personality satisfaction and information, as well as assisting transformation, active techniques are for interacting with soul, invoking soul into personality life. Similarly, purification practices such as *Rainbow Bridge II* [7] and *Coming to the Sunrise*[8] hasten this process by diminishing distortions. Many techniques are designed for specific works, and you will be introduced to a number of these.

Some meditations are rendered truly in service of humanity, i.e., daily meditating upon and speaking the Great Invocation[9] (see Appendix), or regular planetary healing meditations and the Hierarchy Meditation[10] for funding the work led by the holy ones. We will come to understand many wonderful tools for spiritual technology that exist to help us achieve designated ends. The material herein helps us realize our spiritual potential. Quite specific techniques are provided as dedicated readers experience, step by step, both meditation work and the dissolving of barriers that hinder full awakening.

> *As we seek high consciousness,*
> *we are not the first adventurers*
> *or even the first exciting "new agers"*
> *of the group mind;*
> *we are only the current ones.*

Some paths are outer-directed and include a mentor, study, and concentration, as well as union through forms, objects, and symbols. The non-directive approach depends more upon inner guidance; it is more self-directed and expressive with freedom, surrender, and transparency. A third style is receptive, with detachment, emptiness, and elimination as a means of centering, a kind of letting go, helpful in freeing us from daily stress. All forms constitute different approaches to dwelling upon something.

Lawrence LeShan[11] discusses structured versus unstructured activities. In the former we define the inner activity we are working toward and specific activities, such as breath counting. The unstructured form stays focused on a subject and the feelings it evokes. Both are active processes, not passive daydreaming but conscious in intent. LeShan also describes an outer way (with forms, images, and words), a middle way (essentially an emptiness), and an inner way of surrender (observing our own stream of consciousness in a special way). Patricia Carrington[12] talks about non-permissive (strict, one-pointed concentration upon an object) and permissive (a gentle returning to an object of focus when the mind strays).

This brief summary demonstrates that important variations exist in how to meditate. Apparent divergence in classification arises from attention to different aspects of the process.

In these lessons we will explore first the importance of centeredness, then employ the practice of "passive" meditation to assist in building the foundation for a good meditation practice before moving into "active" techniques for their contributions. A systematic approach will provide both "how-to's" and "why's" for your comprehension. As you continue to meditate in the years ahead, you will probably adjust your meditations periodically to fulfill a current need. Most of us find a shift in method helpful from time to time.

From the standpoint of technique, the approach in these lessons will be to assist you in seeing how techniques serve to elevate your practice level by level. After we review the importance of centering and balancing, we will focus for the most part on active, directed meditation, with specific thoughts upon which to focus. Having established the foundation, we will then select a word or phrase—a seed thought—and reflect upon this for a period of time before changing to another. Beginning with lesson 7, volume 1, through the end of volume 2, one such seed thought appears; in volume 3, lessons 1 through 6 will have two seed thoughts. We will cover the relationship to our purpose and the outcome as we proceed.

Techniques alone cannot adequately define meditation, for we are talking about a beyond-words experience, and each practitioner struggles to express how it happens for him or her. We will advance together.

As we think about meditation, we probably hope for guidance or assistance in our daily life. We need to realize we have a body life, a personality experience, and a soul purpose. We must realize there is a point of reference for personality "stuff" and a reference point for soul purpose. Each has something to offer and ways to get there. The reference to receiving guidance for our personal life lies in contacting our higher power, or High Self.

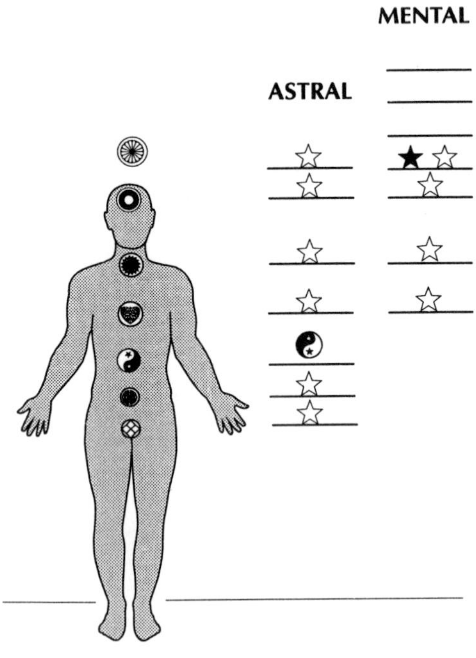

MENTAL

ASTRAL

Figure 6. ★The High Self Guides Personality's Realm. The High Self reigns over the body, emotional nature, and lower mind. When we want information regarding our personality life, we invoke data from this point of consciousness and the ball of knowledge it has collected. The joy (ecstasy) of the mystical experience strengthens or heals weaknesses in the personality. When we hold our mystical experiences in awe (reverence), they assist personality in its alignment to the High Self.

If we use our private meditation experiences to get attention or as fascinating events to relate, we take a valuable encounter (grace, energy) and cloak it in game-playing or illusion, making it a thing of amusement. This not only encases the grace aspect in emotion, making a ball of glamour of it, but prohibits personality from absorbing its energy as the spiritual food of transformation it is designed to be.

Meditation travels the mind-body-spirit information highway. Simple techniques build and blend resources that allow the inner realm to assist our outer lives, such as to battle illness, bring serenity, or access spiritual matter. Comprehending this, we respect the joy of the quiet, the profound, and the beautiful; we build a loving relationship between our inner and outer life. We feel it as ecstasy, appearing almost sexual in nature. However frightening the newborn consciousness seems, we know something transformative is occurring, and we seek those who can be its caregivers.

> Consciousness is transformed when any of the following occur: changes in thinking, world view, beliefs; feelings, motives, impulses, values; as well as altered perceptions, such as heightened seeing (clairvoyance) and sensing (clairsentience).
> —Ralph Metzner, *Opening to Inner Light*

While we struggle in transformation, we usually turn to our mentor for encouragement and perspective. Also, we invoke our High Self to be part of the process by working *"as if," pretending to be soul infused. We wish to create a consciousness of understanding or a response, working "as if" the soul is in control of personality. This chosen perspective has long been used to help disciples rise above the clutches of personality to create a higher point from which to observe. This technique is called working "as if"; the higher point we are building is often called "witness consciousness."

> Jesus said, *I have come into the world as the light, so that whoever believes in me may not remain in darkness.*
> John 12.46

Thus, "Lead us, O Lord, from darkness to light" is the ever-present seed thought of discipleship. As we enter into the maturity of the inner presence time and time again, our relationship to our true Self grows.

As we clarify our purpose, we are better able to determine which process will best deliver us to our destination. Pandit Usharbudh Arya describes three kinds of meditation with exceptionally meaningful designations: 1) Hollywood, for a fit body and eternal youth, 2) Harvard, for scientific study of physiological functions, and 3) Himalayan, for the experience of *samadhi,* "the peace which passeth understanding."

Carrington, on the other hand, distinguishes two primary purposes. "Practical meditation" is designed to enrich the personal experience, to reduce day-to-day problems, and to use centering activities directly for a more fulfilled life. Her second category, "spiritual meditation," demands more strenuous discipline and is designed for spiritual growth.

We would consider passive approaches for enrichment and relief in the category of Carrington's first purpose. As we live in a more centered manner, we meet challenges in a more wholesome way, reducing problems and their complications. Thus we begin to mature spiritually, whether we call it that or not. Active meditation, by our definition, is the more strenuous groundwork for those preparing for illumination.

Similarly, Roy Eugene Davis notes, we meditate for different reasons: for benefits such as peace of mind, increased energy, release from stress, emotional balance; to explore inner spaces of mind and consciousness; and for self-analysis and understanding. He feels the primary purpose is "the intentional directing of attention to the clear aspect of one's own inner nature" in order "to consistently rest in the experience of being."

For every incarnated soul
there exists a learning,
a purpose, a goal.

An expansion of consciousness is happening rapidly now for many. New tools and techniques are readily available to help us meet the challenges of new discovery. A number of recently emerged techniques would be appropriate, among them the MariEl healing work received by Ethel Lombardi[15] and the more recent Cosmic Christ energy received by Jean Kellett and Vera Kaye

Ziverts,[16] which offers training in a series of alignments, a unique method of transfusion with healing, transforming energy. Others receive information regarding use of color and sound for healing and balance. Meditation may periodically reveal glimpses of our purpose or the plan of which we are a part, generally as we determine how to accomplish the previous piece received.

When these experiences happen for scientists or inventors, they are called "brainstorms" or "breakthroughs"; by meditators, they are usually referred to as "glimpses," "insights," "guidance," "aha's," or "I was given . . . . " Regardless of its premise or sphere, let us conclude, "genius at work, an experience of high consciousness."

Practical meditation (for stress reduction, problem solving, and healing), as advocated by medical practitioners, creativity teachers, or mind-expansion proponents, has its roots in religious disciplines, but its purpose differs. The true purpose of meditation and all spiritual disciplines is to realize God in the life of the individual (know the Self) and to attain divine grace. Thus, while we are cautioned not to seek demonstration or tangible effects, desirable by-products often result, such as satisfying relationships, abundance, improved health, and creative output. As others have said, meditation is not an emotional aspirin or a problem-solving technique but, like good nutrition and vitamins, it creates an environment whereby other benefits follow.

> The earliest results achieved will be, firstly, a considerable improvement and control of health and looks, a growing capacity for happiness, an inability to worry or fear, a gaining of popularity, and freedom from boredom.
>
> In time, when greater strides are made, there will be immunity from disease, conquering of fatigue, and prolonging of youth. There will be a growing capacity for helping others, a mastery of sorrow and pain, and the development of healing power. A growing inner force will be felt, both for creating ideas and the carrying out of them.

Defining Meditation Approaches

Passive. A gentle, imaginative, and receptive procedure to "build the cup" mechanism needed to capture the droplets received for conscious comprehension, often the intent of first practices.

Active. A poised, alert state of mind structured to pierce through veils to the quality and essence of thought, a "knowing" technique. The goal is to penetrate the "Cloud of Knowable Things."

Purification. Techniques designed to heal, mend, or cleanse our astral (feeling) and mental ethers of the psychic residue that obscures higher consciousness. Spiritual practices and psychological techniques that dissolve barriers to awareness are for this purpose.

Specific Purpose. These vary greatly: healing techniques, directing energy to others, opening the heart center, sustaining another, telepathy, or other experiential work. Purpose determines technique.

Service. Some meditation work performed regularly as an act of service, love, or commitment to a cause, e.g., visualizing world peace, healing the planet, linking coworkers, invoking resources for spiritual purposes, helping to dissolve fear and panic in a disaster, man-made or natural. Disciples and initiates often serve in this way at a time of transition from age to age, as we are experiencing now in the last years of this century.

Soul alignment is the concept behind all meditation. Techniques evolve as the receiver set is built and expanded to be responsive to increasingly subtle influences. Alignment leads to response to impressions, higher will, and greater love. Thus we take our places in alignment to soul purpose.

> *The soul of man is like to water;*
> *From heaven it cometh*
> *To heaven it riseth*
> *And then returneth to earth,*
> *For ever alternating.*
> —Goethe
> from *Song of the Spirits Over the Waters*

by Carol E. Parrish-Harra, 1993. Permission to copy freely given.

Neither does the tale end here. Very advanced students, such as are the Yogis, become unaffected by heat or cold, wounds, and poisons. They are able to perform feats usually considered as miracles, and they appear to have access to regions of wisdom and felicity undreamt of by us. People of this type move about among us unsuspected. They do not advertise themselves; they are under a Law which forbids them to help unless help is asked, or to give out knowledge unless it is sought and will be properly understood. They are ready and waiting for the time when a growing number of people sense their secrets and beg their help.

—Vera Stanley Alder
The Finding of the Third Eye[17]

Such words encourage our participation in practices little understood. Most of us need all the help we can get. When we are children, we think in childish ways; and while some may feel it is immature to go to God for practical help, most of us do so. In time, we may realize we derive so much from our experience of the Presence, our thinking changes, and we no longer seek demonstrations or proof; we just do the practice and feel its impact as our quality of life improves.

Manly P. Hall[18] identified the purpose as unfoldment achieved by effortless effort (Taoism) through the gateless gate (Zen). Ram Dass sees meditation as a process of awakening, freeing self from the prison of ego. Some teachers speak of destroying ego, but others believe it is possible to attain release from its tyranny while retaining its form for any use we may have of it.

If the ego-self at our personality level is to become a good and faithful servant through which the inner presence, the soul, may freely express, we are not to destroy the ego but to convert it to the service of the soul. Think of this as the spirit training the personality for a greater role: soul infusion.

Where to Begin

Here is a procedure for both relaxing and centering. In an easy, erect position, close your eyes, and focus your attention upon breathing. Mentally observe the breath flowing in and out of your nose. Don't try to control it—just watch. Pause briefly before each cycle, and just watch. As your attention drifts, gently bring it back to simple observation. Do this from three to five minutes. Some people like to count each breath. About eighteen to twenty will be taken in one minute; however, don't be compulsive about the number of minutes or the counting. As you proceed, you will find your body relaxing and your mind quieting. When you can regularly achieve relaxation, you are ready to advance toward meditation.

Do not think of this step as meditation. Allow it to be a centering routine for the physical body. As relaxation occurs, blocks and restrictions (such as tight muscles) ease. Continue now with a five- to ten-minute relaxation as a daily practice to prepare for meditation. Until we master this early procedure, there is little reason to attempt going further. This basic foundation is a meaningful beginning; it changes the body and brings freedom to do more.

> *We need to realize we have a body life,*
> *a personality experience,*
> *and a soul purpose.*

Now we will delineate centering techniques preparatory to meditation. We focus first upon the physical body. Its needs must be met to some degree for it to relax and quit demanding attention. So relaxation allows the body to be comfortable while we shift our focus to the next level of self—our emotional, or feeling, part.

With focus on the breath, note any hidden feelings that may exist behind physical tensions. Be with your feelings, and begin to slow your breathing. Next, locate a spot of warmth in your chest. Breathe into it slowly, easily. Cause a comfortable, warm feeling to expand across your chest and through you, creating a sense of well-being.

The next step is to note your state of mind. As your body experiences deeper relaxation, the energy biocircuit operates more harmoniously and delivers balancing and healing energy to all parts of the body. Later we may realize additional benefits by adding a positive thought. An affirmation of your choice is fine, or I suggest, "I embrace new light, new love, and new peace." Repeat the affirmation in rhythm with your relaxed breaths. Done correctly, a sense of contentment will result.

Whether we truly seek to know in an inner way or not, we may choose to reduce stress and enjoy improved health by merely practicing deep relaxation techniques.

When We Are Relaxed and Centered

When the body is relaxed and centered, we experience healing and rejuvenation. When the emotional nature is relaxed and centered, we experience a sense of unconditional love. When the mental nature is relaxed and centered, we experience peace of mind. When the spiritual level is relaxed and centered, we experience inner knowing.

Relaxation and centering constitute our first level of effort. Practice a relaxation technique for ten minutes twice a day for at least two weeks before proceeding to passive meditation.

Preparation for Centering

We will continue to discuss additional ways to approach meditation. If you are just beginning, you may choose to spend considerable time trying various relaxing and centering procedures. Periods of stress, frustration, and preoccupation with daily living may effectively prevent you from achieving a rewarding practice. In any event, use the preparation techniques, and go as far as you can. That in itself is success. Furthermore, regular use of preparatory procedures will yield amazing dividends in better physical, emotional, and mental functioning. So experiment, and use those that appeal to you even if you do not yet feel you can say you truly meditate.

Relaxation Procedure

To build relaxation skills a systematic bodily relaxation practice is always helpful. The following procedure combines elements from several common approaches.

1. Sit comfortably so you can maintain an erect, easy posture, usually for a longer period of time than is your custom. Attempt to allow the body to operate without distracting tensions, movements, or discomforts while you still maintain an alert mind.

2. Mentally tell the body to "relax and let go." This usually cannot be done simply, so attend to parts of the body systematically.

a. Direct attention to the forehead. Try to feel any tension in that area. If you cannot feel the area, wrinkle the forehead, and hold it tightly a few seconds. Then, let it go. This gives you a kinesthetic awareness of what it feels like to relax. After a while, you become sensitive to minute degrees of tension and will not need to tighten the muscles first.

b. Now attend to the muscles around the eyes. Do the same as with the forehead; squeeze the eyes tightly shut. Be aware of the tension, and when you let it go, be aware of the difference.

c. Move to the jaws, and do the same. Then check the throat area in the same way. Now move to the shoulders and neck, and relax those.

d. Repeat with the arms, first one and then the other. You may need to relax the upper and lower arm separately. Instead of tightening the muscles in the arms, just begin to lift them, but don't do so. Feel the trace of tightening necessary to lift, then let go.

e. Repeat this with the stomach muscles, then with the hips.

f. Relax the legs separately, first the thighs (begin to lift and feel the traces of tension) and then the calves. Tighten the feet and then relax them; feel relaxation flowing through all parts of each foot. Wiggle slightly, and relax.

3. Now slowly let your attention drift back up and over the body, starting with the lower legs. Notice any tension in the muscle groups you have relaxed previously. If you feel any

rigidity, tighten and then let go. You may be surprised how much tension has crept back into a few muscles. By the time you reach the forehead, you should be quite thoroughly relaxed.

4. Remain in this state for a while. Let your mind drift over the body to monitor how well it is staying relaxed. If an area has tension, let it go.

This procedure may take fifteen to twenty minutes or more at first or if we are under unusual stress. When we are nervous or under great tension, learning to relax will reap future rewards with any meditation style. Substitute this for meditation for a time.

After conscientious practice, you will develop a greater awareness of even mild tensions any time you choose to attend to the body. You will be able to loosen whole areas quickly and completely, or you may even relax the whole body at once upon mental command. Practice does make perfect.

Centering Procedure

The following breathing pattern does much more than center us. It works to improve internal balance, reduce stress, and promote rest and serenity. When we are particularly upset or scattered, it may well be used as preparation to meditate. Or it may be practiced alone to enhance general well-being.

The basic process is to inhale for a set number of seconds (or slow counts) and hold the breath for half as long as the inhalation; exhale for the same number of seconds as the inhalation, and hold for half the count. Begin a new cycle immediately.

The breath taken should fill the lungs comfortably but without strain. Fill the lower lungs first—this feels like filling the abdominal area—then the upper lungs or the chest. Count mentally to eight for the inhalation, hold it for a count of four; exhale for a count of eight, hold for the count of four. Repeat five to seven times, or more if you wish. Do not strain. Breathe easily and normally through the nose, and take a comfortably full breath. Doing this evenly and slowly will prevent dizziness or hyperventilating. Such exercise is particularly helpful for enabling you to relax, so you might use it both before your relaxation process and for a calming effect before going to sleep.

Conscious breathing invites the spirit (breath) into the personality. Continuous inward and outward breathing is recommended in several techniques. While each breath technique has its appropriate use, different practices have different goals.

Not many people have had an opportunity to study *Western Yoga. Peter Roche de Coppens, a friend and a fine teacher, had studied the esoteric tradition since young adulthood when he met Roberto Assagioli. When Peter went to Iran to study the teachings of the Zoroastrian tradition, he learned the Western Yoga postures, known for health-giving properties that prepare the physical body to facilitate etheric energies. He states that this series of twelve postures has influenced all traditional Western calisthenics.

Some Western esoteric systems discourage *Hatha Yoga for its tendency to create energy overload and congestion in the etheric body, suggesting the body itself is now sensitized sufficiently so that the primary chakras do not need additional stimulation. Dance, sports, or calisthenics are to replace Hatha; however, relaxation and centering exercises still should be practiced. Perhaps they are needed in this stressful era even more than in the past.

> Hatha yoga is millions of years old. It was used in the Lemurian Race to bring fusion between the physical and etheric bodies, making it possible for the command (the wish or desire), the volition of the man, to be passed immediately to the nervous system through the nadis, the etheric nerves. This purpose was fulfilled ages and ages ago. There is no need for it today. Pranayama, the science of breath, is even more dangerous than Asana. Breath is fire and the best way to use this fire is in normal, deep breathing. We need no other breathing exercise than this.
>
> —H. Saraydarian
> *Cosmos in Man*[19]

Different systems, for specific reasons, use different numbers of breaths; the numbers have significance and correlate to the systems. My first teacher used the seven breaths to greet the day because there are seven planes and each breath reminds us we are drawing life, **prana,* to the physical all the way from the cosmic Source. Western Yoga generally uses a seven-count in its exercises. Other systems use eight because it is the number of power and strength. Do not be confused, but follow what becomes comfortable. Most systems count half of the inhale/exhale number for holding.

If all this seems too much, begin your day by just facing east and taking several deep breaths to align to the energy of the sun and the new day. You will see quite wide variations of this idea. The Maya daykeeper, Hunbatz Men, has provided an exercise for saluting the sun from that ancient tradition. Facing the sun, hopefully with its rays on your face, speak "K'in" seven times. The tongue is placed behind the front teeth and a bit of a click sounded as each tone begins. Hold the tone for the length of a breath, invoking the energy of the sun into your being. The technique, offered as a part of the *solar initiation, is also used for solar meditation. The masculine sun energy creates one stream of planetary energy; the feminine moon energy is the other. In the world of nature the *Cosmic Christ draws from both streams to maintain wholeness and balance in nature and even within our matter-nature. We are familiar with this inner energy as yin/yang.

It is important to realize the potency of breath and breathing exercises. We should not presume that breath work holds no power since we breathe without thought. Be gentle and respectful of any and all breath work, exercising or training only under the guidance of an experienced mentor.

Wonderful thoughts may be added to our daily attunement: gratitude for our blessings, love of life, requests for healing of self and others, invoking help, energy, and light for the day. We need to acknowledge the power of the day, noting our opportunity to breathe in the prana accessible to us with greater awareness and new appreciation.

Exercising the body is an extension of meditation. The physical body, as well as heart, mind, and soul, deserves care and respect. A meaningful saying to remember here: *A well-exercised body does not hold depression.*

Your first assignment

Soulstar Relaxation Procedure

1. Read a brief piece of devotional material.

2. Use preparatory chanting, singing, or background music while you begin to relax.

3. Become still, and close your eyes. Use your opening gesture as you imagine a light shining upon you from over your head.

4. Spend a few minutes relaxing your body in a comfortable position. (Do not lie down or lean against anything.) Concentrate upon becoming as relaxed and centered as you can. Breathe deeply. Feel a light shining upon you, and allow this light to flow into you.

5. Now visualize yourself enclosed in this light. Feel its vibration or quality.

6. Allow the light to penetrate deep into your being.

7. If your mind wanders from the awareness of the light in which you are enclosed, re-form your imagery. Gently refocus, and begin again.

8. After a few minutes, return to an awareness of yourself—personality and the light interacting to illuminate the essence of your nature.

9. Express your gratitude for whatever you have experienced.

10. End your experience with your chosen closing gesture.

You are ready for Level 2

Suggestions for Responses and Questions

To derive the most value from this course, you are encouraged to correspond with the meditation tutors at Sancta Sophia Seminary to receive the benefit of experienced assistance. Meditation tutors, knowledgeable people with extensive experience, offer each person enrolled in the meditation course individual attention. They will answer questions, provide guidance and helpful suggestions. When the following enrollment form is submitted, it provides tutors with background information so they may advise you appropriately, and they will respond with directions for participation.

When to best send this request will vary. Generally, before writing, you need to have completed lesson 2, or nearly so. Any time you wish to express a thought, share an experience, or ask a question, we suggest you make notes while it is fresh in your mind. This may even take the form of a diary or journal. But, unless a particularly urgent situation arises, reserve it until you have completed the exercises for a lesson. Then mail your notes to the meditation tutors. The reason to delay your response is that many times what you are experiencing or wish to express will expand considerably during the work with a single assignment.

If you have a question or critical problem that needs answering before you continue your meditations, or if you have an exciting happening to share, send that immediately as a separate item, labeling it "special request."

Complete the application on the next page, please, and advance to lesson 3.

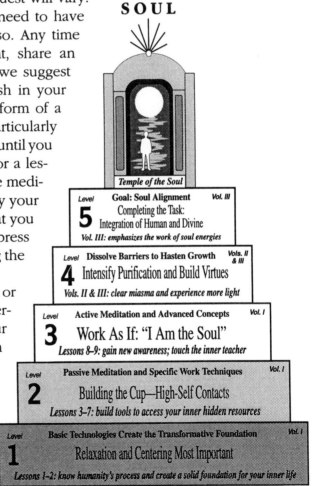

SOUL

Temple of the Soul

| Level 5 | Goal: Soul Alignment | Vol. III |
| Completing the Task: Integration of Human and Divine |
| Vol. III: emphasizes the work of soul energies |

| Level 4 | Dissolve Barriers to Hasten Growth | Vols. II & III |
| Intensify Purification and Build Virtues |
| Vols. II & III: clear miasma and experience more light |

| Level 3 | Active Meditation and Advanced Concepts | Vol. I |
| Work As If: "I Am the Soul" |
| Lessons 8–9: gain new awareness; touch the inner teacher |

| Level 2 | Passive Meditation and Specific Work Techniques | Vol. I |
| Building the Cup—High-Self Contacts |
| Lessons 3–7: build tools to access your inner hidden resources |

| Level 1 | Basic Technologies Create the Transformative Foundation | Vol. I |
| Relaxation and Centering Most Important |
| Lessons 1–2: know humanity's process and create a solid foundation for your inner life |

Please copy this form, complete, and mail to the tutoring committee. This data is held in confidence. It is designed to help tutors serve you in your journey to high consciousness.

Meditation Correspondence Course Enrollment

Name (Please print)_____

Address_____

_____Phone (_____)_____

Date of Birth (month, day, year)_____

Gender_____Place of Birth_____

Occupation_____

Marital Status_____

1. Why do you want to take this course?_____

_____

2. What is your current understanding of meditation?_____

_____

3. Have you ever meditated?_____If so, with what group and in what way?_____

_____

4. When did you begin to meditate?_____

5. How long do you meditate?_____How often?_____

6. Do you try to maintain a pattern—same place, same time, same technique?_____

7. How much time can you give this study?_____

8. Are you easily distracted by outer stimuli?_____

9. Do you tend to glance at the clock to see if the time is up?_____

10. Do you skip your meditation time on slim excuses?_____

11. Do you try to make up omitted meditations at a later time, or let them go?_____

12. Is guided meditation (one led aloud by someone else) easier for you?_____

13. Do you discuss your techniques, experiences, findings, or reactions with others?_____

14. When you hear of the experiences of others in meditation, do you feel you must be doing it wrong or that you aren't "as advanced" or "as spiritual"?_____

15. Are you ever discouraged and tempted to "forget the whole thing"?_____

16. Give a brief summary of the experiences and problems you have had with meditation. (Use additional paper if needed)_____

17. Have you ever practiced seed-thought meditation?_____

18. Have you used drugs: hallucinogens, alcohol, marijuana?_____

For how long?_____With what effects?_____

Do you now?_____To what degree?_____

19. Have you had psychic or ESP experiences?_____If yes, please describe.

_____

20. Are you familiar with Alice A. Bailey, H.P. Blavatsky, the Agni Yoga teachings? What level of exposure have you had?_____

21. Do you have significant racial, religious, or other prejudices of which we need to be aware?_____

22. What is your educational background?_____

23. Have you read the New Testament?_____the Old Testament?_____

24. Do you belong to a church or religious, metaphysical, occult, or meditation group?_____How long have you been affiliated?_____

25. Do you have a creative activity?_____What is it?_____

Note: Any other information you wish to share is welcome. You may use additional paper for your answers.

Date_____Signature of Applicant_____

Enjoy exchanges with a mentor who will provide personal attention and written responses to your meditation lessons. The enrollment fee is $5, and written assistance and guidance to deepen your spiritual life is $15 per submission. Please pay the $15 mentoring fee each time you submit correspondence. Mail to: Meditation Tutors, Sancta Sophia Seminary, Dept. **M11,** Sparrow Hawk Village, 11 Summit Ridge Drive, Tahlequah, OK 74464-9215.

Levels of Meditation

Read not to contradict and confute,
nor to believe and take for granted,
but to weigh and consider.

—Sir Francis Bacon

Y ou have probably already discovered that your meditation sessions are not the same from day to day. As you study and practice regularly, you will experience various levels of intensity. Authors organize and label these stages a little differently, as may be expected, but by seeing what several have offered about meditation, you will begin to grasp many qualities of experience difficult to express.

Only after learning to relax are we ready for passive techniques. We must be tranquil and receptive to the next step: directions, visualizations, and thoughts. Performing such exercises helps us experience deeper levels of ourselves, to ignite out-of-sight awareness, visualize, and receive droplets of new insights. Considerable personal growth may be experienced through the use of guided work. However, *the most important aspect of passive work is to build the cup, the receiver set, the mechanism for catching impressions* we contact both now and later.

Often procedures that could be divided into preparatory activities (relaxation and centering) and stages of meditation themselves are popularly termed "meditation." After all, meditation is not an all-or-none state of consciousness. The Yoga Sutras of Patanjali[1] was one of the earliest attempts to provide a systematic guide to enlightenment. This process has been passed on for hundreds of years in the oral tradition.

Patanjali described three levels: concentration, meditation, and samadhi, seemingly natural steps in building the mental mechanism. Concentration organizes material in the conscious mind as it explores the subject upon which it focuses. Concentration techniques increase focus, creating the ability to narrow, sharpen, and lift to higher contact, while insightfulness, just noting everything about ourselves, leads to expansion. Meditation, however, penetrates the form and adds new awareness. When we transcend the object and pure meaning is experienced, this is samadhi. Although these levels are described separately, they work together to produce perfect contemplation.

Of the basic spiritual practices of the Western way—prayer, adoration, meditation, and contemplation—we generally are taught prayer and adoration first, awakening a rush of energy in the emotional (astral) body to lift the attention toward higher centers of consciousness. Prayer energizes the heart (fourth chakra) and engenders positive energy. We generally think of this as love and our prayer as communication with the Source. While prayer is to soften the heart, adoration thrusts us toward achieving oneness (toward the highest chakra, the crown). Prayer creates the emotional focus to lift us heavenward.

Chanting is sung prayer, bringing us the same benefits and more; it can also balance energy centers and create an acceptance of healing. Passive meditation uses this sensitivity to build a receptivity to impressions which may come in response. Having captured the impressions, we contemplate. Now we grapple with the thoughts, insights, or guidance received. In meditation we seek the contact that happens when our mind and the All-Knowing Mind interact. That contact initiates a downpouring of spirit awareness.

We have then two emotional activities: focusing on the heart prompts a flow of devotion that lifts us into action, and adoration comes in response to contact with our spiritual self. Similarly, we have two mental processes: meditation and contemplation. Concentration and contemplation seem like meditation, and yet we define meditation as that central experience of it all, the contact point, uniting concentration and contemplation. Contemplation is the term used when a soul-infused person "thinks" in the presence of the Greater Light, allowing her- or himself to be assisted in the process by even higher influences.

The Value of Contemplation

The mental unit registers only that which is contemplation. The conscious contemplation of experiences, seed thoughts, and situations transfers the subject—from rote experience held by the permanent mental atom to awareness reached or lessons learned—into the developing mental unit. Permanent seed atoms in the physical, astral, mental, and spiritual planes register all happenings, conscious or unconscious, to be carried forward to be energized again when we are being prepared for another birth.

These seeds and their constant refinement travel with us, retaining all we have gathered from our earthly life. All experiences, good and bad, remain here as a complete history called the *akashic record. We register change in ourselves now and in the seeds by living a conscious life, eliminating to a high degree living mindlessly or acting out old programming. At each level of our nature, we *choose* and we *practice* discipline and awareness. We seek to be consciously present in all situations, emotionally responsive, mentally alive and registering input, creating well-considered responses in light of our spiritual concept of life itself and in light of the highest point of consciousness we recognize at that particular time, which may be either the High Self or later the soul (*solar angel).

MENTAL

ASTRAL — contemplation
adoration meditation
devotion

Figure 7. Four Disciplines Practiced by All Major World Religions.

Prayer is a deliberate attempt to center ourselves in conversation with God, the highest power and principle, or with Jesus, as a divinely led teacher, or the Master for whom we have strong personal feelings. Others may focus on different revered figures: Mother Mary, the representative of the divine feminine, a saint, a teacher, or holy one. Catholicism and orthodox Christianity have retained more of this more esoteric understanding than have most Protestant denominations. Theosophy, Rosicrucianism, and other approaches have also reintroduced in their philosophies perfected beings who assist humanity. The primary focus of Spiritualism, a lesser known denomination of Christianity, is contact with both lesser and higher evolved beings in the spirit world.

We focus and form thoughts to pray. We broadcast our message to the universe for the higher, more perfect consciousness to *hear*. In the silence of meditation we give up our confusion, our anxieties, our personality manifestations. Quiet and open to the flow of life, we allow peace to move through our being. We become centered in the flow or the inner self. We frequently discover a similar state in observing God in nature.

Another way to describe the process within the emotional-feeling nature: 1) We focus upon the heart, 2) positive energy flows, and 3) our attention moves higher. 4) Contact with the holy allows the outpouring to permeate our expanded nature. 5) We experience a spontaneous rush of great love as a natural result of communion with the Source in adoration. 6) After adoration, we rest in holy consciousness and feel/know we are loved.

ASTRAL

☆
———
———

☆
———
emotion
———

Figure 8. Levels of the Feeling Nature. The natural progression in the astral nature is from emotion to devotion to adoration. Prayer stimulates the heart and expands devotion. Adoration stimulates the highest level and draws us upward from heart (prayer level) to aspiration (guidance level).

MENTAL

Figure 9. Levels of the Mental Nature. Similarly we can relate what happens in meditation and contemplation within the mental nature. Here our conscious mind chooses to meditate and be receptive. The star to the left represents the placement of High Self, the guide of personality, and the star to the right represents solar angel's influence at its lowest point of vibrating "mind stuff." The organization of higher levels of mind occurs as the mental body is both formed and organized (O). This process is what we know as the *Path of Initiation.

conscious mind

Through guided meditation, we build a mind screen, steadily becoming accustomed to following the images, staying centered and open. Subtle feelings and thoughts may register as impressions. Gradually the cup is built, and new levels of consciousness will be achieved. In our meditation we use the light of the soul, or higher consciousness, to examine our grasp of reality. This study is called contemplation. The proper use of insight, awareness, discipline, and study is exercised to hold the mind clear and focused as other levels of self are stimulated, to a greater or lesser degree, according to our personal ability to respond to incoming influences. Utilizing this openness, the higher world pours forth blessings to help the initiate comprehend and advance in developing his or her expanding potential.

In contemplation we think about a subject or principle in order to become totally aware of it with all our understanding. History records that St. Anthony, often called the "Father of the Desert," established a school of meditation using rather systematic procedures. From the year A.D. 310, his teachings have guided thousands to the path of meditation and, to this day, time for meditation may be found on the schedule of most monasteries and convents. As it is commonly taught in monasteries in the Western world, meditation is not the freeing experience taught herein but "actively thinking upon." In its highest form, contemplation is used in our method after we have connected with an aha/realization to help us integrate the new awareness (volume 3). It then, in fact, facilitates the organizing of new levels of abstract mind. In her booklet, *Contemplation,* Helen Brumgardt calls contemplation "the activity of mystical consciousness."[2]

So, even within developmental stages, we see that recognizable levels of consciousness exist through which the individual must ascend. With the higher experiences of samadhi, we neutralize destructive tendencies of both the feeling nature and the mind. These higher experiences lift us in the direction of a more complete unity. *As long as we have any consciousness of God as apart from ourselves, we are not in samadhi.*

This Oneness is the intent of all meditation work. We use meditation as the doorway to the Holy of Holies; we enter for a personal embrace. Historically, such access has been gained through the heart by devotion and through the mind by expansion of consciousness. Ultimately, our intention is to synthesize; we link heart and mind to "thinketh in the heart," and then lift this refined mechanism for soul infusion.

This brief description leaves so many unanswered questions, it may be rather puzzling. That is to be expected since we are trying to express in a few words the results of humanity's long history of delving into the fundamental nature of the mind and the cosmos and their interaction. It helps to envision yourself as a cell floating in the sea of the cosmos. We are usually aware of boundaries around our mind, but boundaries dissolve in samadhi and we experience the wholeness.

Much of what we experience in inner realities becomes almost impossible to put into words. Since meditation provides such a variety of experiences, let us look at ways others have attempted to describe these realities.

Roberto Assagioli,[3] psychiatrist and author, identifies three levels of self-realization. The first shift in awareness expands our sense of being, of aliveness, a perception of what constitutes a greater value to us. Assagioli's definition closely relates to how we see ourselves functioning in the world. A second, even higher level is the inner experience of pure self-awareness independent of any ego content or function. The third and highest is the realization of the spiritual self. The latter two levels require meditation to be experienced.

Assagioli recognizes a distinction between conscious self (the "I" consciousness of personality) and the High Self. His "I" differs from the outer ego and its functions at the first level of self-realization he describes. We will call this level High Self and acknowledge its goal to provide guidance for the developing ego. We will also acknowledge this as integrated personality or personality-made-ready. His pattern is basically equivalent to several yoga systems as he provides a Western technique for describing and defining consciousness.

Hugh of St. Victor, an early church father and the first of the great Victorine mystics, wrote that a spiritually awakened person has three eyes with which to see: "the eye of flesh" (physical), "the eye of reason" (mental), and "the eye of contemplation" (spiritual).[4] Just as our physical eyes see people and objects, our mental mechanism perceives ideas and concepts. Lastly, as we escape the limitations of ego and experience perceptions of a higher reality, we see with the eye of the spiritual self.

> In the Indian yoga teachings, we find a different meaning given to the notion of three eyes. Here the left eye is lunar, related to night, the feminine, the receptive; the right eye is solar, related to daytime, the masculine, and the dynamic-expressive. The vision of these two must balance and alternate rhythmically. The third eye, in the center of the forehead, was regarded as the eye of inner vision, intuition, and clairvoyant perception, when awakened through meditational, yogic practices.
>
> —Ken Wilber, *Eye to Eye*[5]

Wise ones have always recognized the presence of senses that link us to the beyond. Just as the eye has its spiritual connotations, so too does the ear. In Luke 8.8 we find, "He who has ears to hear, let him hear," and in Ezekiel 12.2, "Son of man, you live in the midst of a rebellious house, who have eyes to see and see not; who have ears to hear and hear not; for they are a rebellious house."

> Ancient dissectionists spoke of the auditory nerve being divided into three or more pathways deep in the brain. They surmised that the ear was meant, therefore, to hear at three different levels. One pathway was said to hear the mundane conversations of the world. A second pathway apprehended

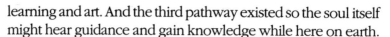
learning and art. And the third pathway existed so the soul itself might hear guidance and gain knowledge while here on earth.

—Clarissa Pinkola Estés
Women Who Run With the Wolves[6]

Manly P. Hall[7] distinguishes three aspects of unfoldment: meditation (inward contemplation of divine realities); realization (the understanding and acceptance of divinity and divine purpose in all things); and illumination (conscious at-one-ment with the universal principle). The first is essentially a tranquil state, but we achieve realization and illumination by conscious disciplines.

The realization level, that deep flow of thought we reach in active meditation, correlates to our "aha's" when synthesis occurs—again, frequent in active meditation practices. Think of illumination as a cosmic consciousness experience. Little conscious thought is involved; one breaks free and just is, just knows.

Lawrence LeShan[8] discusses "four major paths" of meditation. Number one strengthens personality structure through the intellect. Two, the path through emotions, extends caring and expands feelings. Three, the route of the body, includes Hatha Yoga, T'ai Chi, Sufi dancing, and Western forms for developing sensory awareness. Four, the path of action, whether service or *karma yoga, includes total concentration on whatever we are doing. Just as these paths appear to be ways of meditating, they also imply levels in the sense that our practices affect the depth of reality we may experience.

Several authors use adaptations of Patanjali's three-fold classification: concentration, meditation, and contemplation. In his discussion of Hindu meditation, Bradford Smith[9] adds a preliminary stage of withdrawal of the senses before one-pointed concentration. We could compare this stage with our preliminary procedures of centering and relaxation.

Christmas Humphreys[10] expands the three stages by discussing lower and higher meditation. The beginning-level work assists in dominating the lower, separative self and developing the mind's higher faculties as preparation for spiritual unfolding. The higher level relates to samadhi, beyond intellect. To him contemplation is a level about which little can be written without distortion, the "utterly impersonal awareness of the essence of the thing observed." He specifies that these levels work together to produce the desired state of consciousness known as meditation.

While training the personality and the study of higher concepts are spiritual disciplines and practices that prepare us for transformation, the purpose is for all aspects to merge into the experience of meditation. We stimulate the shift in consciousness by lifting our expanding nature toward the soul, which then magnetically draws us the rest of the way. Thus, there is a part *we* cannot do. We go as far as we can by conscious action; then we must surrender and allow ourselves to be lifted into the greater experience of Oneness. To encourage the idea that *we* do it creates a problem. If we try harder, do more, push, or never let go, we create blocks.

> Do not depend on the hope of results. When you are doing the sort of work you have taken on . . . you may have to face the fact that your work will be apparently worthless and even achieve no results at all, if not perhaps results opposite to what you expect. As you get used to the idea, you start to concentrate not on the results, but on the value, the rightness, the truth of the work itself. Big results are not in your hands or mine. All the good that you will do will come not from you, but from the fact that you have allowed yourself, in the obedience of faith, to be used by God's love.
>
> —Thomas Merton

From time to time we will be embraced by the Great Oneness. When it subsides, we vibrate with love, freedom, beauty, and joy: this is *grace,* the gift of samadhi, the afterglow of an experience of high consciousness. In meditation we learn to "wait on the Lord," comprehending in a wonderful new way.

Lama Anagarika Govinda,[11] a Buddhist teacher, discusses four "movements" in meditation. He believes it is important to release the role of the intellectual observer into the experience of deeper reality. He illustrates with the process of breathing. In between the outgoing and incoming breaths comes a turning point, a moment of stillness: "the inner and the outer world become one." Since this "no-point" exists without a fixed identity—it cannot be called inner or outer—we have a point of pure beingness, beyond thingness.

Thus, in the first meditation movement, we free ourselves of the perception that we are "points" in isolation, recognizing outer as the physical side of universal consciousness. Buddhism calls this "Mirror-like Wisdom." When we begin to realize we are not different from the essential nature of all living forms, the second movement starts, that realization of oneness of all life, the "Equalizing Wisdom." This must go beyond emotional realization so we may understand that true organic wholeness demands form and differentiation, as well as the common essence.

Such awareness leads to the third movement, an acceptance of the infinite interrelatedness of all, without losing the distinctiveness of each. This "Distinguishing Wisdom" leads to intuitive consciousness of an inner vision. All three wisdoms lead to a fourth movement of meditative experience identified as "All-Accomplishing Wisdom," or the "Wisdom That Accomplishes All Works." This movement brings the wisdoms into daily experience so we may lead lives of selfless, *karma-free action with compassion and understanding.

Govinda wonderfully characterizes the "flow." The ouroboros is an ideal symbol: "Everything runs in a circular motion."

Figure 10. Ouroboros. This cosmic serpent, depicted with its tail in its mouth, is the symbol of the manifested universe in its cyclic aspect of completeness. The feathered serpent of the Western wisdom tradition symbolizes the primordial unity that encloses all time and space. As the serpent encircles the all, it represents wisdom contained.

In each of the above examples the process of meditation is approached differently, but as we progress through the lessons, it will become clearer that meditation penetrates successive layers of mind. In our quest for the underlying reality, we become more keenly aware of different qualities of consciousness enriching our understanding and awakening our intuition. In this course we will provide you with a method to penetrate deeply into ultimate reality while acknowledging that, as this happens, it also becomes a way of transforming our perspectives on daily living.

Brain-Wave Cycles

These early lessons have sought to help us become aware of different layers of the mind imparting different qualities of experience and providing keys to assist us in understanding the foundations of meditation.

Let us not forget the light at the solar plexus. This first light of mind, called the quiescent self, was developed by evolution itself: the generic human seed. The function of rational mind depends somewhat upon calming our emotions enough to think, a most important step in the mind-building processes. Today, however, because the left hemisphere of the brain is so highly developed, many people suppress their emotions and heed only the rational mind. Now we are to attempt to bring right hemisphere into balance with left.

We register the contact of right and left hemispheres through the feelings of the solar plexus before we can translate its message mentally. When we slow the brain-wave activity and move from beta (30-14 cycles per second) to alpha (14-7 cycles per second), we become more imaginative and the ability to sense and perceive is stronger. When brain-wave frequencies slow to 7 cycles per second, we drop into theta. The 8-10 brain-rhythm cycle per second is considered a natural healing range. The positive influence revitalizes and lets energy flow from the astral plane through the etheric and into the physical. This in turn increases our sense of at-one-ness with the world about us. If we drop into the lower ranges, we generally do not retain impressions, but other benefits are many. Below 4 cycles per second, we are in delta, asleep.

Contact with right hemisphere or inner reality that we are able to remember is considered alpha and upper theta. Guided meditation capitalizes on our ability to experience here and to draw from the High Self as we continue our attempts. As we have seen, meditation systems may endorse different techniques and have various models, but they all basically agree that by going inward we find the doorway to higher levels of reality beneficial in stress reduction, health building, and different ways of knowing.

Persistence builds a track that becomes better defined and more easily traveled. We learn to escape the turmoil of lower mind, usually dominated by the ego and, in time, come to know our spiritual nature.

The practice of meditation as outlined in these lessons combines simple disciplines which increase our sense of self-worth with an understanding that makes us want meditation and realization to be a part of our lives. Through this approach, we achieve gradual, natural growth in a dedicated and transformative manner as we advance toward becoming soul-infused personalities.

The most important aspect of passive work
is to build the cup, the receiver set,
the mechanism for catching impressions.

In your effort to gain as much as possible from a meditation practice, you may run into a few common problems. After all, the books we read—even these lessons—set lofty aspirations. When we envision where we are going and what to expect, we tend to want it all right now, or at least in the very near future. However, results come in their own ways with experiences unique to each practitioner.

Love of productivity can result in too much "push" or in trying to hasten development too intensely. A more beneficial attitude is to embrace your meditation practice as "entering a process." If we think of our meditation deepening and transforming us, gathering momentum and energy and serving us each time, whether or not we are able to measure productivity, the experience will ebb and flow with its own benefits. A hard-to-define cumulative effect occurs. Simply put yourself into posture, do what you can, relax, and allow. As one stage leads to the next, your life will be vitalized to transform. Sooner or later concern about productivity abates, and we meditate for other than self-centered reasons.

I cannot too strongly advise students against the following of intensive meditation processes for hours at a time. . . . The average aspirant is so sensitive and finely organized that excessive meditation, a fanatical diet, the curtailing of the hours of sleep, or undue interest in and emphasis upon psychic experience will upset the mental balance and often do irretrievable harm.

—Alice A. Bailey, *The Externalization of the Hierarchy*[12]

When too much effort is applied to the meditation process itself or when we try to drastically alter our lifestyle in too many ways at once, hindrances occur. On the other hand, some systems involve such long-term exercises and practices that we may despair of accomplishing it all even in a long lifetime. In the beginning, we meditate 1) for help, 2) to heal pain or problems, 3) to increase spirituality. In time, we meditate because the maturing personality desires interaction with the evolving soul.

Lifestyle Changes

If you have been meditating for a period of time before starting this course, you know that lifestyle changes seem to occur with the process, often so subtly you hardly are aware of them until some happening brings them to your attention. Others are instituted consciously in a desire for a more holistic life, in harmony with the goals of meditation. We come to know eventually that meditation is a way of life.

If you are new to meditation, you will profit by realizing that what you habitually think, feel, believe, and do influences your personal development. Progress can be enhanced greatly by harmonizing your thoughts, feelings, and behaviors with the insights you find through spiritual studies and the key discipline of meditation. So from time to time, we will provide suggestions you may wish to adopt. In this lesson we will mention several directions your life might take; in subsequent lessons we will be even more specific.

Exactly what is needed to change our lifestyle depends upon habits of thinking and acting developed through the years. A great deal of what we think or believe, our emotional reactions to various situations, our moods and how they flux, daily patterns of action, our general emotional attitude toward life—all are outgrowths of essentially unconscious mechanisms. *Maya is a term used to describe the "glamours, illusions, and delusions" perceived by limited mind, the world of appearance. We tend to react as our environment has shaped us rather than from any conscious, reasoned choice. Meditation makes us more conscious, freeing us from conditioned responses.

At different times, we may be asleep, half-awake, or awake, but the goal is to become more awake, more aware. Having been hypnotized by cultural and social codes, in order to revive we must endeavor to dehypnotize ourselves. Now we are stirring. When we evaluate our conditioning, we retain some old ideas and find others no longer work for us. We eliminate some and remodel others. Before we arrive at an enlightened state, we struggle with periods of awake and wonderful versus operating by rote with little conscious thought. And, we realize how often we vacillate between these extremes.

Think of the search for truth in this way:

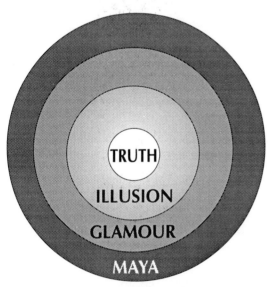

Figure 11. The Search for Truth. We must work our way through rings of obstacles, discovering the truth within or the truth that works for us at a given time. This course is designed as a principal guide through the barriers to high consciousness that exist for most. It has served extremely well, and combined with the suggested meditation practice, it will prove transformative for you.

We suggest you make no drastic or sudden changes in what you eat, how you act, how you use your time, or how you respond to your friends and family. This is exactly what some do, hoping to speed their progress or because they think they must in order to be "spiritual." Inevitably they find they must become less intense and even reclaim much of what they thought they had left behind. Study the suggestions in these and related materials, trying them to see if they fit your needs. You may find them even more useful at a later time, an excellent reason to read the lessons a second or third time.

Most students find it beneficial to read with regularity spiritual material designed to inform and inspire. References used in these lessons are valuable, but many books from around the world contain wonderful guidance. The Holy Bible and other religious books are fundamental. Many spiritual courses taken in connection with meditation provide reading lists. If you would like suggestions for materials in a specific area, ask your tutor. A good time for devotional reading is upon awakening in the morning as preparation for the day, as well as just prior to meditation. Before going to sleep, clear the mind of the day's heaviness and cares with spiritual reading.

Inspired reading lifts our minds from worldly matters to those of spirituality. We would suggest in addition *Mystery of the Christos* by Corinne Heline,[13] *Song of God* (the Bhagavad Gita with commentary by Swami Venkatesananda),[14] and *The Aquarian Gospel of Jesus the Christ*.[15] This type of reading is so rich, we need only small measures to realign our minds, to relinquish everyday thoughts and cares, and to be prepared for inner reality. All of these may be ordered through the Village Bookstore.

The Nightly Review

Retrospection is another useful procedure for mind clearing. The following exercise has an ancient history as an important discipline in many traditions. Simply put, it is recalling the events of the day in reverse order. Vera Stanley Alder calls the process the "nightly review."[16] Others use the term "evening review" or "daily review." By doing this, we keep our attention on the corrections we choose to make in our daily life.

This nightly review is designed to expand consciousness and help us see and correct areas of our own behavior, automatic reactions, attitudes, or habit patterns detrimental to our spiritual growth.

In effect, we are reviewing the astral pictures etched upon the ethers. We go into the memory of the event, call it up, and reconstruct "the file." Challenging? Yes, but wonderful. *The law of karma isn't designed to torture us but to provide reason to change our consciousness.* Karma pushes us to learn "this causes this, and that sets that into motion." It isn't ten pounds of pain in return for our having caused ten pounds of pain; it grants as much push as it takes for us to be ready to change our consciousness to a new perspective. By integrating a new understanding of daily events, we are enabled to create new responses.

In this exercise, we review our day backwards. If we note a response or experience we wish we had handled differently, we re-create the drama as we wish the situation had unfolded, playing it out line by line, meeting the challenge and rewriting the event according to the wisdom of our higher nature. This does two things: it predisposes us to make things as right as we can, and it alerts us to patterns of which we are unaware, where we, in fact, jump track and fail to abide by our newly formed, improved awareness.

Reenacting the happening in our mind shows the basic self how we wish we had met the challenge and thus provides a pattern of desired behavior for the next similar happening. We may have to repeat a painful experience several times to break an old habit, but each time we use the nightly review, the new way becomes more real and available. Our consciousness changes, and we neutralize the karmic pattern. Hurrah—step by step we learn a better way!

One more vital point about the review and rectifying errors or ignorant responses: as we put our new and better understanding into daily practice, we learn to *live* the new life, not merely intellectualize about it.

Another important benefit: as we practice regular reviews, we accomplish work which otherwise would be left until our death. After death, we move through the *bardo, as it is called, to review the astral pictures and evaluate in the light of high consciousness what has been accomplished in our life. In the solemnity of the moment, we will see and perhaps regret not having changed matters by learning new responses earlier. So, as we are doing this work, we look at our personality and train ourselves to put our principles into daily practice as best we can. We seize this opportunity to change our life consciously and significantly, rather than postponing the review process until death. This hastens our spiritual growth, or what is meant by "taking heaven by storm" rather than waiting for the unconscious evolution of humanity. We thus move forward in the process and become an advanced thinker working for the good of all.

Assessing the happenings in reverse keeps us from rushing through event after event and overlooking significant symbols or details; situations will appear different than when they actually occurred. Note your feelings as you recall these events, but limit the review to about ten minutes immediately before retiring at night. As you replay the events in a purely descriptive way, remain calm and passive, withholding any emotional reaction. Pay particular attention to experiences that jump out at you. Be aware but not involved.

This exercise needs to be as objective as possible, or it will deteriorate into a self-defeating process. Should it develop into a reminder of all the things we did wrong or did not do as planned, it may create guilt. Try to be non-judgmental about yourself, others, and events. This awareness helps keep recurring patterns from slipping unwittingly into your unconscious. Do not be compulsive about recalling every single detail, or you will overemphasize events, make too much of a single incident, and perhaps be up half the night.

We do not want to avoid recognizing guilt. We have a need to feel guilt when it reminds us we have violated our code of ethics. It is the destructive effects of *excessive* guilt from which we would be free, that terrible overriding guilt that damages us emotionally and crushes hope.

What will this nightly review do for us if we use it appropriately? Many things. It will help us become more conscious of the facts of our existence, as distinct from our automatic responses and emotional coloring. Frequently we gain a new perspective or insight regarding the incident. Thus, we increase our freedom to choose to live more consciously, rather than imprisoned by habits. If we see something clearly involves a need to forgive and release another or ourselves, we can choose to do so immediately, not merely forget it or continue to stew about it. We face and accept the situations that trouble us instead of tucking them away in our subconscious, pretending they didn't happen or were different.

By clearing the mind daily, we truly start each day afresh. Living more in the here and now develops consciousness and delivers us from the nagging by all that has occurred in the past. We cannot alter the events, but we can change our reactions and neutralize much of the negativity we experience. While we do not want to suppress habits, events, or information, we can learn to release the past and free ourselves to deal with the present in a more up-to-date, day-to-day manner.

How do we know we are using the technique appropriately? The results will be clear in most instances. We will advance through the process smoothly and rapidly. Sleep will follow quickly. We will begin most days refreshed and eager. We may discover a new feeling of freedom. Meditations flow more effortlessly and creatively.

If we are judgmental instead of descriptive, we will find we are stalled or stuck on an event. We will worry rather than finishing the retrospection and going to sleep. As we recall a situation that needs more thought or action, we put it on tomorrow's agenda and release it. (We will discuss dissolving barriers to enlightenment in volume 2. It is important to have constructive ways to release situations, people, and things.)

Another helpful insight to our nature is achieved by noting how we get up in the morning. Reluctantly? Bit by bit? No good until that cup of coffee or other hot drink is downed? Try this. First, stand up and inhale slowly and deeply; hold the breath briefly, then exhale through the mouth with some force. Do this three times.

Next, do a few stretching exercises. While inhaling deeply, stretch your arms above your head—reach for the stars. Hold your breath as you slowly bend as far as you can to the left and then to the right. Exhale as you lower your arms. Now, inhale deeply again, hold your breath, extend arms out to the sides, and twist from the waist—first to the left, then to the right, three times. Then, exhale. (If these exercises make you dizzy at first, do them gently.)

Now bend over gently and stretch toward the floor, exhaling as you bend and inhaling deeply as you straighten. Do this three times. Last, do five or ten half-squats, and lift your arms high, inhaling as you come up. Then exhale as you lower your arms and half squat. By this time, you will have the blood circulating and the energy flowing.

Now stand quietly a few moments with your arms upraised and spread; feel the energy of the universe flowing into you; consciously express your thanks for another day. These few, brief minutes will add joy and vitality to your living and generate a more rewarding meditation life.

By blending meditation and a few spiritual disciplines, we construct a framework for a reasonable, effective approach to a sensitive daily lifestyle that encourages our best natural tendencies. Balance comes from a kind of thinking which suggests broad and deep potentials. As we explore each experience, we open to higher influences. This on-going process challenges and enriches life.

As the nature of the bird is to sing, the nature of the maturing soul is to express itself, linking personality and inner nature to daily life.

Assignment

Practice the Nightly Review

Before retiring, see how well you are now able to relax. Report to your tutor, please, on your relaxation results and your use of the nightly review. Having selected an event for review, here are some helpful approaches.

Relax. Speak the Om softly and gently, and retrace the day's happenings. Move backward through the evening and into the day to a troublesome event. Not everything needs equal attention, but some incidents stand out. Settle upon any incident you wish to remodel.

See the setting as it was, and recall the cast of players. Prepare to *gestalt. Who set the play into motion? You or someone else? Do you remember what was said, the rush of feelings, the moment where a thought or awareness could have created a wiser outcome?

Now construct a new scenario from one moment before the event. At the moment you were in a position of creating a possible future sequence of events, you chose one (consciously or not); now you are choosing another. Imagine you are the director cutting a segment of a movie that is a bad "take." Now rewrite the script in a way more acceptable to your spiritual self.

Redo the "take" step by step. Forgive yourself and others. Affirm the good behavior you have selected, and rest in peace. Thank your higher consciousness for bringing this to your attention and for the insights you have gained. Affirm your ability to create appropriate responses under the guidance of your own high consciousness to any challenge you meet.

Be peaceful in heart and mind, realizing your inner creative power assists you every day to live a life of goodness and joy. Through you, the soul seeks to express love, wisdom, and service. As you regularly do the nightly review, these principles will integrate themselves more and more into the activities of every day.

At this time I suggest you begin to keep a journal that notes these three simple points. We are taught that as we awaken to the inner nature, we are promised three occurrences daily. We must train our spiritual eye to see them. Ask yourself:

- Where did I have an opportunity to do service today?
- Where did I meet my challenge today? Did I see it as it approached, or did I fall into it?
- And, where was my blessing today?

Reminder: Are you ready to register with the meditation tutors? Refer to the registration form just before this lesson.

Building the Cup

*To realize God as immanent
is to discover God in the center of your own being—
the subject of yourself.
To realize God as omnipresent is to discover God as the center
of all other beings and all which has being—
the subject of all objects. To realize God as transcendent
is to realize God as the source of all subjects and objects—
all being itself—and to realize God as the source which will abide
when the entire cosmos in all its levels of creation
and all its life forms has passed away . . . .*
John White, *The Meeting of Science and Spirit*

As a spiritual teacher, I would say meditation is more than an illusive subject—among the most difficult to articulate because it is a perceived experience, not an intellectual process. We seek to encounter that part of our nature hidden from our conscious mind, yet we tend to think the conscious mind is "us." In the meditation process, we attempt to let go and allow the parts to become a whole. Thus, meditation, the foundation of all self-unfoldment, is not just expanded knowing but expanded *being.*

Meditation is the fundamental self experiencing the energies of the universe. We learn to attune to the flow of the universe to restore the energies or frequencies we use in our lives daily. Just as sleep refreshes the body, meditation revitalizes the personality.

The physical results of meditation have been evaluated in excellent fashion by the Transcendental Meditation[1] group. And the Silva Mind Control[2] approach provides an excellent introduction to levels of consciousness defined by brain-rhythm cycles per minute, a logical explanation that can be meaningful to some. They use many psychological, scientific, and philosophical terms and are not meant to be religious approaches. Both have provided research that is well documented and quite interesting, especially if you are planning to teach this subject.

Robert Ornstein in *Psychology of Consciousness*[3] uses the terms "right headed" and "left headed" to distinguish between approaches. The left-headed person describes the usually dynamic "outer" approach of the achiever; the right-headed describes the more contemplative, sensitive, intuitive approach of the artist.

Biofeedback is a technique by which the participant tries to consciously control bodily functions previously believed to be involuntary; it helps people shift from one hemisphere to the other as desired. This trick of balance and interaction between hemispheres of the brain is a goal of meditation. To be a "balanced being," happy and expressive, but also in touch with our divinity, is the ultimate experience for all humanity.

Our meditation technique must be geared to our lifestyle, religious views, daily schedule, and even whether we approach life logically or intuitively. These interconnecting themes of life patterns make it impossible for one technique to work for everyone.

Several universal methods have developed through the years. Let us look at them. These approaches are based upon focusing or concentrating upon a basic "sense" and penetrating inward through it. Each of the five physical senses may be used as a focus to take us inward, concentrating our attention upon the chosen sense until we become transfixed and can ignore messages from outer stimuli.

Seeing: visualization magnified until we lose touch with other senses and pass through this level into another reality: mandalas; focusing on candle flames; icon-gazing; guided meditations.

Hearing: lost in sound by filling our awareness to the exclusion of all else: mantras; chanting; repeating the name(s) of God; sounding bells or gongs.

Feeling: so aware of the sensation of touch, all other awareness is crowded out: massage; pain; sexual ecstasy.

Smelling: lost in aroma or odor to the exclusion of other senses and consciousness is altered (remember the oracle at Delphi): incense; pungent potpourri; the unfortunate practices of inhaling gas fumes or sniffing glue.

Tasting: hallucinogenic state induced by ingesting herbs or plants: peyote; coca leaves.

In the emerging mental techniques, the way we are developing currently, the most common ways of centering (a term introduced by the Quakers and often used by psychologists) are:

Chanting. The mind is given a simple melody and brief words to play with or to produce as a concentration tool. Listening to the piece causes the hearing sense to dominate, while other data-gathering mechanisms are turned off and peace and harmony are restored.

Visualizing. We look at or image in our mind a picture, an icon, a candle flame, or a flower until we merge into a sense of oneness with the image.

We will apply a variation of this imagery as we use guided approaches in passive meditation. When we paint as artists, work clay with our hands, or weed the garden until all awareness of the outer world is lost, we become centered by focusing our touch. Regardless of how centering is achieved, we discover great calmness following total concentrated effort.

We may undertake rote tasks intentionally to produce a change of consciousness. Washing dishes, shelling peas, or polishing glass may serve as tools to help us make this shift. Driving mesmerized (though dangerous) is familiar: "highway hypnosis." Dancing has long been recognized for this—especially whirling, the device of the whirling dervishes, or the stomp dancing of Native Americans.

*T'ai Chi, an ancient moving meditation from the Orient, is becoming increasingly popular in the United States. Hatha Yoga can become a form of meditation as it relaxes the conscious mind and lets the inner awareness take precedence. The old-fashioned

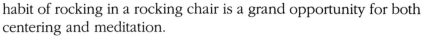

habit of rocking in a rocking chair is a grand opportunity for both centering and meditation.

When we are engrossed in a project and the telephone rings, we are often startled. We may feel we've been "jerked" back to the outer world. This indicates we have been in an altered state of awareness or at least not in our usual "tough enough to deal with the world" attitude.

To be interrupted abruptly while involved in meditation can be a nerve-racking, even painful experience. Most teachers recommend precautions for comfort, such as the phone off the hook or a sign on the door ("sleeping" or "do not disturb").

Meditation is a conscious attempt to become one with our inner nature or self. This idea has been and will be expanded by spiritual people to signify becoming one with the God-Within. To a non-spiritual or non-religious person it may mean becoming centered with the inner potential or creative nature. To others it is a moment of perfect peace and serenity wherein we achieve renewed comfort and strength. Restored and refreshed, we begin life again with new energy. If we perceive God as infinite energy and place no limit on our potential as we become one with the divine creator of all life, we may think of meditation as our "refueling time." We attune, and we listen to the guidance of the Inner Presence.

Most Christians have been taught to pray, or at least to respect prayer, all their lives. In the early Christian community, however, meditation was a spiritual practice just as widely supported. Master Jesus often retired from the multitudes to the quiet and urged his followers to "seek the Father within" or "enter the silence."

In the Old Testament we find many references to meditation. The psalmist was particularly inclined:

I meditate far into the night; I communed with mine own heart; I have examined my soul . . . .

Psalm 77.6

My mouth shall speak of wisdom; and the meditation of my heart shall be of understanding.

Psalm 49.3

My meditation of him shall be sweet: I will be glad in the Lord.
Psalm 104.34

If we are dense manifestations of God consciousness, in returning to our inner life, we encounter God, our Source. If we, the outer personalities, are imperfect and troubled, it is possible for us to move inward to a more perfect manifestation; in that space we truly "become one with," reestablish peace, and rediscover our perfect pattern.

> If you read "Jesus ascended to heaven" in terms of its metaphoric connotation, you see that he has gone inward—not into outer space but into inward space, to the place from which all being comes, into the consciousness that is the source of all things, the kingdom of heaven within. The images are outward, but their reflection is inward. . . . We should ascend with him by going inward. It is a metaphor of returning to the source, alpha and omega, of leaving the fixation on the body behind and going to the body's dynamic source.
> —Joseph Campbell, *The Power of Myth*

Since most of us will have some difficulty bringing to conscious mind the treasures of the deep inner self, it is best done by establishing a definitive practice to help us. All of nature meditates naturally. When we daydream, we are going inward spontaneously at the call of imagination, or because of boredom. The difference is that now we want to be able to shift levels for a definite reason and at our command.

What are some good reasons for spending our time this way?

1. To escape from mental pressure; to restore harmony and peace of mind.
2. To relax the body; to aid healing or rejuvenation processes.
3. To increase creativity. When we release thoughts from the conscious mind, we often become more aware of the whole. "Think time" for business people is an approach gaining recognition in today's marketplace, especially for executives. Creativity is a highly sought attribute.

4. To gain new insights. Inventive solutions often appear as we experience the silence, and data may flash into the mind during or after our quiet time.

5. To be strengthened and calmed to better confront the experiences of daily life, bringing beneficial effects to our psyche.

And perhaps the best reason of all:

6. To know the will of God, as holy people of all traditions have always sought. In a world besieged with stress and demanding outer expression, such practice is of great value when it helps us sustain our faith, find the beauty in ourselves, and align with our chosen ethics.

Today, life affords us few opportunities to "be in touch" with our inner nature. In times past, humanity lived under less stress. Few of us today have time to spend long hours working in the garden, swinging on the front porch, or strolling down peaceful lanes to admire nature's handiwork. Yet this kind of simple activity has soothed and comforted people as they move through their stay on the Earth plane. Rushing highways, achievement goals, tight schedules, competition, social demands, and stressful situations take a toll on group sanity. Living close together further exacerbates our problems.

Recognition of the need for meditation and its freeing effect on our consciousness has given rise to a variety of methods. Not all meditation techniques require that the eyes remain closed. Zen Buddhists, for example, emphasize the necessity to be in touch with reality by keeping the eyes open. The consciousness still becomes centered, brain-wave activity slows, and the same healing wholeness occurs.

Please refer to *Meditation in Christianity*,[4] a valuable book for students seeking to understand Christianity's ties to the East. Remembering Jesus was from the Mideast and considering the customs of that time and place, this work provides new appreciation for Master Jesus as the great master teacher of the Christian tradition. Meditation is one of the basic practices of both East and West. The process you have begun has led many to experience much.

Down through the ages, the East has placed a major emphasis on meditation. While the practices of the yogi have attracted attention, this has not helped people understand them. Perhaps perceiving God as intelligence unmanifest will help us see the picture. We might also image the process as going into a tunnel that grows smaller and smaller, becoming more tightly focused, until suddenly we break into an inner chamber of brilliant light. The action is one of focusing, and yet, at a perfect time, it spontaneously expands into the inner sanctuary of awareness, an inner reservoir "beyond words," just as God is beyond words. We recall, as soon as thought is expressed again, we have left the meditation experience of samadhi.

> *Meditation is the fundamental self*
> *experiencing*
> *the energies of the universe.*

As we return to outer consciousness, some of this vast awareness may be pulled together into thought, but the strengthening and restoring effect registers beyond words—in the Christian tradition, "grace."

Thus meditation leads us beyond the conditioned mind into the state where mind is free to be drawn into higher thought. As a discipline, meditation is touching the source energy; it is returning to our essence. Familiar phrases today are "raising our vibrations" or "becoming centered." And as we do so, a change of awareness or an altered state occurs.

Common Questions

Frequently we are asked, *If I pray, do I need to meditate?* I like to define prayer as talking with God. When we pray, we focus our attention on what we want to say. When we meditate, we establish time for a reply. We must believe we are sending a message telepathically to the all-knowingness of God, or we needn't bother to pray. If we are going to express our love, list our needs, or give our thoughts, it also seems we should wait for the answer. If any of us were able to arrange a hearing with the President of the United

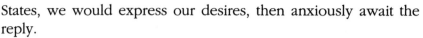

States, we would express our desires, then anxiously await the reply.

Throughout the Bible it is written, "The Lord said . . . ." Let us think about this. In what form did the Lord speak to the prophets and leaders of his people? Don't you imagine it was from within them? Meditation then is being receptive to the outpouring that comes from our Source.

We send messages to the world about us every day, every hour, without speaking. We telepathically dialogue with the Great Life whether we know it or not. This is the "thoughts are things" concept, that "all is mind" awareness in daily life. Prayer is the consciously focused time we create to send the message we choose. It may take hours or only an instant. We need to ask ourselves: Do we expect the conscious moments of prayer to offset the rest of the thoughts we send? Or, are prayer and the focus we create designed to lead us into a lifestyle in harmony with our prayerful choice?

Is it Christian to meditate? St. Paul acknowledged this inner presence of divinity: "Do you not know that you are the temple of God, and that the Spirit of God dwells in you? . . . for the temple of God is holy, and that temple is you." (1 Corinthians 3.16,17)

A recurring symbol in the Bible for meditation is the word "silence."

. . . a time to rend and a time to sew; a time to keep silent and a time to speak.

Ecclesiastes 3.7

Keep silence . . . and let the people renew their strength.

Isaiah 41.1

The Lord is good to him who waits for him, to the soul that seeks him. It is good for a man that he should hope for both the truth and the salvation of the Lord. . . . Let him sit alone and keep silence, because he has laid thy yoke upon him. Let him humble himself, for there is hope. Let him turn his cheek to him that smites him; let him be filled with reproach. For the Lord will not forget for ever.

Lamentations 3.25-31

Why do people speak the Om? All religious traditions acknowledge the power of sound, the Creative Word. Deemed the generative first word or tone that vibrated through the receptive void and shaped a response, Om continues to be used as a materializing power, spoken with clear intention and deep concentration.

Om—pronounced home without the h, and both letters prolonged—is the first and foremost syllable of the ancient, sophisticated Sanskrit language. Om is the foundation word and principal power word of the Upanishads, the most revered writings of the Vedas, the oldest scriptures known.

> *It is often said,*
> *the universe knows two words,*
> *"Yes" and "Om."*

Considered the sum of all vibrations of the universe, Om is said to be the sound of God we hear in meditation, the witness to a divine Presence, the sacred Word that was issued by God to create all that is. The Word also recreates and restores God's presence in lives and in creation. This power tone invokes and restores the divine to our lives individually and collectively; it is a healing force to bring peace to the world.

Sometimes spelled and pronounced "Aum," the *Om* of the Vedas comes to us in the sacred word *Hum* of the Tibetans, the *Amin* of the Muslims, and the *Amen* of the Egyptians, Greeks, Romans, and Jews. In Hebrew it means "sure and faithful." Christians usually translate *Amen* as "so it is" or "so be it." An esoteric translation, "and so I affirm," is an active, participatory proclamation, not a passive agreement.

People and groups of an inclusive nature tend to use the tone to consciously connect to the divine expression behind all religions and traditions.

Giving voice to this sacred tone holds a special place in the heart of an awakened one. Paramahansa Yogananda said that when we become attuned to the cosmic vibrations of Om, we actually vibrate with it whether we know it or not. *It is often said,*

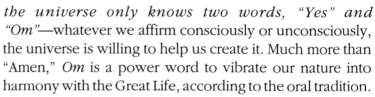

the universe only knows two words, "Yes" and "Om"—whatever we affirm consciously or unconsciously, the universe is willing to help us create it. Much more than "Amen," *Om* is a power word to vibrate our nature into harmony with the Great Life, according to the oral tradition.

Due to their vibrating frequency on the astral plane and the connection to the sound current, words have a more powerful impact, positive and negative, upon us than we may realize. Spiritual students traditionally choose to ignore negative words and seek to integrate the beneficent into their practices.

Other words are also of great value for their potency. "In the name of _____" reminds us of the power of names; disciples are often gifted the privilege of invoking in their Master's name. Words of power originating in one tradition are often adopted by others because the energy bestowed is recognized universally. Examples are *Shanti* (Hindu), *K'in* (Mayan), *Shalom* (Hebrew), *Mir* (Russian), *Aloha* (Hawaiian), and *Ho* (Native American).

Each power word creates an energy that ignites waiting seeds of karma within the speaker and seeks to do so in the external environment as well. Each of the above may be spoken as mantras. Used for its propensity to affect matter, "Heal," spoken with force, breaks up crystallization in the astral to free energy for rejuvenation or realignment.

While every language has a variety of power words or phrases that may be adapted for mantric use as the serious student is ready, any word so used must harmonize with its user to be beneficial; then it will work to clear away the debris that encumbers life. It is not unusual to state and restate, "light, love, and power," or "I am love, I am peace, I am joy." While these expressions, spoken with intensity and intention, may become power words, the most universal in its nature is the *Om*.

Does everyone need to meditate? Is it a personal choice? These questions are important because they remind us of the difference between "need" and "desire." So often humanity must review its needs as opposed to its desires.

Let us turn our thinking to Abraham Maslow's concept of the Hierarchy of Needs. Maslow stresses how different human consciousness is at various stages. He points out that just as food at one level and shelter at another are absolutely necessary, love is as well. As we master our needs at one level, another set of needs, equally important for the next step, comes into being. When self-respect and respect from others are as essential as food, self-esteem becomes a necessity of life.

Not everyone needs to undergo the same processes for self-actualization. Some need to pit their strength against outer measures: i.e., money, physical prowess, possessions. As we realize success in attaining one level, we find a natural restlessness urging us to a further goal, one subtler and more challenging.

In this period of exaggerated materialism, we hear of people of great wealth, power, or success radically changing their customary pursuits toward creativity, peace of mind, spirituality. Newspapers, novels, and television witness to this hierarchy of needs influencing people's lives. Some truly need to be fulfilling other interests. Let us examine these stages for a better appreciation of the differences.

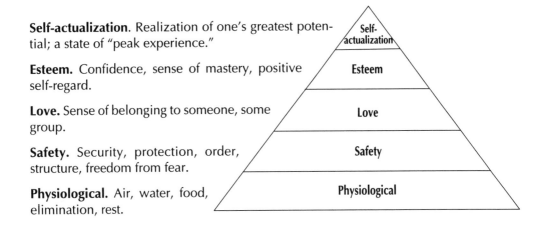

Self-actualization. Realization of one's greatest potential; a state of "peak experience."

Esteem. Confidence, sense of mastery, positive self-regard.

Love. Sense of belonging to someone, some group.

Safety. Security, protection, order, structure, freedom from fear.

Physiological. Air, water, food, elimination, rest.

Figure 11. Maslow's Hierarchy of Human Needs. The higher needs which appear to arise in man after his basic survival needs are met are the result of an inner pressure toward a fuller expression of being, a self-actualization, in the same naturalistic sense that an acorn may be said to be pressing toward an oak tree.

—Abraham Maslow, *A Theory of Human Motivation*[5]

81

The technique of transcendental meditation was seen by Maslow and his contemporaries as a means of achieving extraordinary human growth, creativity, and fulfillment. He postulated that first humanity must satisfy its survival needs, bringing into play a natural quest for personal comfort and selfish indulgence. Only when we are secure in our physical survival can we seek power and opportunity to express our desire for higher fulfillment. Only when these needs are met will self-actualization, the great prize, be sought because it is at this stage that we develop the desire to sacrifice for the Self. Humanitarian interests, causes, and high creativity now assume great value for us, and meditation and spiritual practices begin to demand expression.

The Emerging Soul

When the nature we call "soul" emerges, seeking illumination, enlightenment, redemption—an expression of its own natural, impersonal, clear wisdom—Oneness begins to infuse our personality. Our lives begin to reveal a relationship to all life previously hidden. This oneness is illumination. It brings enlightenment to our experience of life, redeeming personality and revealing our divine origins. Personality becomes the clear vessel that serves as a focus for the light of high consciousness we call the Soul.

An old adage of importance in spiritual teachings is *we cannot give up what we do not have.* We often think it should be easy for another not to be so attached to what we see as having so little value. Wisdom teachings help us understand questing as gaining consciousness (ball of knowledge) that we may present to the higher nature. We give the prize we have won to that higher awareness; we surrender it to the Inner Lord. We build a strong and capable ego, then clear it of glamours and illusions so we may have a personality with healthy self-esteem to relinquish to soul infusion. The hard-won prize, self-actualization, is the process of understanding and fulfilling the self, activating awareness to express freely through personality, allowing greater self-determination. In

Esoteric Christianity this is the Christ-Within standing revealed, or advancing on the Path of Initiation.

Mystical experiences sharpen our focus as we move toward more divine awareness. This is what spiritual life is all about. The experiences of prayer, meditation, contemplation, and other disciplines encourage the process. When we decide consciously to meditate, we are deciding to discipline ourselves, to participate deliberately in our own growth process. We are throwing the weight of our conscious mind behind the naturally evolving process to become "whole," choosing to become "one with it all," or "holy."

In the meditation experience we discover inner space, we journey into ever-new levels of self. The only way to get from here to there is by doing, and that is what this study is all about. Guided meditations—passive—provide students with a variety of experiences. They are designed to facilitate the unfolding of the inner nature. The process is to relax and merely allow yourself to be led by the sound of the leader's voice, inward. Follow directions, and permit yourself to experience the non-physical. No one really can say what will happen. There are no guarantees, but the first step is to agree to experiment in a safe setting. Have no expectations. Allow your imagination, the image-making mechanism, to be free. Evaluation or review will be done later. Whatever occurs and its value need not be determined in advance. Right now you are simply allowing another level to come into being in order to see what it has to offer, if anything.

Please recall, the process we recommend is:

1. Prepare—dim the lights, take the telephone off the hook, choose a place in which to have the experience.

2. Become comfortable—turn inward by a conscious effort; stay relaxed, quiet.

3. Become centered—you will come to know this as a "feeling" place along the way.

4. Concentrate—image the exercise following the directions.

5. Be in the quiet.

6. Gently return to the outer world. Breathe, and adjust outward.

As frequently happens in meditation, we do not know we are approaching the void. We cannot tell what is going to occur beyond a certain place of centeredness. As we leave the center source of our being, conscious mind takes the reins and begins to know again. We recognize we have been to the Source. We feel new strength, awareness, and peace within our nature. We return more secure, more loving, restored to the outer world. We cannot compel this richness to occur, but we rejoice that it has.

Experiential Exercises

Some people find wearing a pair of earphones to listen to music a wonderful experience. Adjust the volume to just a bit louder than usual. Close yours eyes, and sit in a manner to which you have become accustomed. Can you become lost in the experience? Perhaps sound is the way you will find most effective for you.

Experiment with lighting a candle and looking at the flame. Some people recommend a darkened room at first. (After you feel the effect of this technique, you will find it successful whether you are in a lighted room or in the dark.) When we focus our attention upon the flame itself, observing the dancing, flickering motion, a magnetic trigger seems to pull us inward.

Another time, fill a plain (design-free), clear bowl almost to the top with tap water; then stare into the water. After a few moments, your eyes will tend to off-focus. Allow this to happen, and you will find yourself becoming lost inward. You will sometimes have impressions, thoughts that come to you out of nowhere, or perhaps you will find yourself returning from inner space.

If visual techniques such as these do not work well for you, as you seek to explore meditation further, you might try imitating just ordinary daydreaming. Look at the sky. Watch the movement and design of the clouds. Practice creating the feeling of daydreaming: looking, off-focusing, drifting, becoming centered through the freedom of movement, then coming back.

An oriental technique is to look into a flower. Something very nice happens, as though the concentration upon that beautiful object pulls us so that we see a similar beauty in our own nature. Nature has always been a major gateway through which we find peace, just looking at or merging with a tree, a flower, or a lovely scene. For many individuals, the awesomeness of mother nature helps God become a part of their lives.

A spiritual training technique through the ages has been to meditate upon paintings or tapestries. Think about this, and realize how easy it is to be seated, to look into a scene, and to find yourself a part of that scene.

In mystery schools of old, the students, as initiates, concentrated and meditated upon symbols, as well as scenes. For example, they might meditate upon a host and chalice and unexpectedly "see" the host turn to light. It has been recorded that such practices produced powerful visual mystical experiences.

In the Western world we have a tendency to listen to words or tones. In other traditions, such as the American Indian and the African, drumming, as a technique, is structured to produce a vibratory frequency within the body and to generate a rhythm. The rhythm has a centering effect. Chants are much the same.

Let us think about this just a bit. Let us sit down, become very comfortable, and say a mantra over and over, such as, "I am one with God, I am one with God, I am one with God." As you repeat this, the only awareness you hold is to the words; then you begin to lose the words, forgetting your place. This shows that another influence has interrupted the pattern. Yet there is no outside interruption. An inside alteration is pulling you more deeply into your center. Repetition triggers this mechanism, especially in rote prayers, such as The Lord's Prayer or Hail Mary. This is the reason devotions such as the rosary are said in a repetitious, sing-song manner.

In the Eastern tradition one *experiences* chanting, and I choose the word "experiences" carefully because it describes what really occurs. The words and tune of a chant usually are short and simple, and repeated again and again. The mind settles into its course and continues to go on because we are committed to sitting in this place and doing this for a period of time. The nature of such activity causes us to become bored with the externals: the sitting, the music, the simple words. Without outside stimulation, centering happens, at which time the body may begin to move or sway or rock

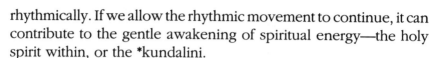
rhythmically. If we allow the rhythmic movement to continue, it can contribute to the gentle awakening of spiritual energy—the holy spirit within, or the *kundalini.

It is not out of the ordinary to become so centered during our chanting exercise that we lose the words and become still. We're not singing, we're not talking; we're just resting in the center of it all for a few moments. We will soon find ourselves coming outward, again experiencing an awareness of what is around us. We may feel a loss of time if we stop to think about it. However, in a chanting structure, there is usually little or no awareness of timing. Nor are we as aware of the timing as we are with the music.

You might want to try simply focusing upon a picture—an icon of Jesus or Mother Mary or any scene that awakens devotion within you. Any of these are appropriate tools, just as symbols are, or closing your eyes to visualize the deity of your devotion.

As we make meditation part of our lives, we choose the most helpful time of day. Many people enjoy meditating first thing in the morning. Others find that taking a shower and getting dressed, being a bit more awake, improves the meditation experience. They are more alert and adjusted within for the focusing work ahead.

It is rather widely agreed by meditation teachers that there is also a need in the afternoon, somewhere between five and six o'clock, for a second meditation break. For those returning from work, it provides a nice change between the work-a-day world and the evening at home. Taking a few minutes to rebalance seems a good way to reestablish our center and release the stress and confusion of the day, to prepare us again for entry into the home or the evening activities. It may take some evaluation and schedule rearrangement to discover just how you wish to accommodate a personal meditation time in your life.

It is *essential* that you are not impatient about your routine. The most important part of the process is in "just doing." In the beginning, any sense of excitement or newness blocks the way, so simply relax, and have your quiet times until you have trained your body to be still and your mind to enjoy the routine. Then it will begin to happen!

For additional training at this stage of development, refer to the *Meditation Plus* and *Experience New Dimensions* audio tapes cited in lesson 1. Use *Meditation Plus* first. Following one tape of meditation guidelines, five tapes (two sides each, thus ten exercises) will provide the experience needed by those building passive meditation skills. Most people need to master passive meditation prior to beginning the seed-thought work of active meditation. These tapes furnish exercises to facilitate building the receiving mechanism and experiencing specific inner work designed to introduce you to new capabilities.

Remember, the purpose of passive meditation is to build the cup—the receiver set—and to develop our extended sense awareness. Just as we have our five physical senses, we have subtle senses with which to gather information about our spiritual reality. These senses are already working for us unconsciously, in our imagination, whether we know it or not. Close your eyes, and pretend you are peeling an orange. You can smell it. How? Through the psychic part of yourself, your extended sense awareness. Psychic is defined as "of the soul."

When we taste, smell, feel, see, and hear in our dreams, we draw upon our nonphysical senses to portray the story. Passive meditation is a process designed to stimulate this part of our nature while awake but in an altered state of consciousness.

These exercises use the nonphysical senses to build the mind screen. As we develop our image-making mechanism, we learn to cast pictures upon it. We begin by using our imagination, but once we become accustomed to using the mind screen, the spiritual self is able to cast its impressions upon it independently.

Thus, with passive meditation, we activate our spiritual mechanism and then assume a position of receptivity so the nonphysical nature can impress personality. It is an important level for sensitivity development. Here we slow the brain-wave activity from beta to alpha or even theta as we withdraw our focus from the outer and refocus upon the inner part of life.

We must remember that fears, phobias, old pictures, and associations have also been impressed upon our awareness. All impressions are not valid, and thus we must work to clear our psychological levels of distortions. In these three volumes, we call these "barriers to be dissolved." They present challenges on the way to illumination. Specific techniques, as well as meditation and other tools of purification, are suggested to eliminate these obstacles, and as we do, the quality of daily life is enhanced greatly, as you will see.

Recognize the potency of *thoughtforms. The old often arise to haunt us; these shall be healed, but now it is time to use thoughtforms well. See yourself healthy, happy, bright. When in doubt, create positive thoughtforms. Carefully choose your words, and as you study, recognize the "goodness" of the food with which you nourish your mind. Watch for any signs of a negative attitude toward yourself.

We endeavor to create thoughts, feelings, and a body in such alignment to the evolving self that the silence and peace, the light and love, the grace of the self flow freely in our personal life and as a source of illumination for others. Silence and peace do not mean a life without challenge. That is a total misunderstanding of spiritual teachings. In Mark 13.12, we read, "Brother will deliver his brother to death; and a father his son; and the children will rise up against their parents and put them to death." It is that the more enlightened live in peace as they meet challenges, knowing the trials are important for themselves, for the group of which they are a part, and for the evolution of humanity.

Accept necessary, inevitable pains without undue resistance and without adding to the negativity. Accept in a positive, increasingly peaceful manner while practicing nonresistance.

Continue your exercises with relaxation and centering. The following meditation is passive in nature and designed to increase awareness of our relationship to the Holy. Remember, "It is within me and I am within It," or "The Deity and I are One." This is an excellent meditation to free oneself of negativity or resist negative influences. Practice this exercise more than once before reporting the results to your tutor.

Assignment

Opening to My Personal Deity

Close your eyes, and prepare yourself for an inner experience. Relax. Truly see yourself as you are today, and let go of all barriers, facades, protective defenses.

Allow yourself to become very simple, pure. Feel the child-within. Acknowledge your weaknesses and needs, the imperfect areas of your life or body that need the healing touch. Feel your vulnerability. Think, "I am the creation of God, my Source."

Be a little child again. Remember the spiritual command to be as a little child—simple and unprotected before him.

Visualize the Lord, your Master—your spiritual inspiration, whomever it may be. Visualize that one reaching out a hand to touch you.

Become receptive. Feel love awaken within your heart, pouring through your body and mind, awakening the divinity within you. Receive the message of love, and experience your loving response.

Allow love, warmth, enthusiasm, divine inspiration, the fervor of renewed spiritual commitment to flow through your being.

Accept this key, this touch of Godliness, to enrich your faith, to inspire and guide your own spiritual development. It will encourage you to move forward in your life with the inner knowing that you and the Father are one.

Hold the divine love now flowing within to guide you to new awareness of peace on Earth and the heaven within as you feel your own purified nature responding to the touch of your personal Master or inspiration.

Be still. Feel your oneness with Divinity.

For this new beginning, the goodness of this day, the unfolding pattern of our lives, we give thanks. So be it.

Opening to the Kingdom Within

I am the light of the world.
You are the light of the world.

John 8.12 and Matthew 5.14

B y now, you have begun "to reunite with the living stream of consciousness and creativeness . . . ."[1] The depth and nature of your experiences may vary considerably from others taking this course. Whatever yours have been, cherish them as your unique responses. Probably you have now begun to appreciate the process as one of gradual unfolding, rather than dramatic, overwhelming, or instant change. Regardless of the intensity of your responses, we will proceed more deeply into the nature of meditation and suggest ways to enhance your total experience so that you live more fully aware.

These discussions of meditation suggest its depth and complexity. Additional concepts derived from both wisdom teachings and experience will provide you with a substantial informational base, enabling you to place your own experiences in a broad frame of reference and maintain a stable perspective.

It may already be clear to you that meditation is not to condition our minds but to free us, to liberate us from compulsive functioning of mind and body or habitual emotional responses. The fact that this release actually occurs in advanced meditators has been demonstrated by research.

Psychologists and physiologists describe a phenomenon of *habituation* which is characteristic of ordinary consciousness. Simply stated, exactly repeated stimuli tend to reduce our reaction to them. This is true at unconscious, as well as conscious, levels, such as our reduced response to habitual noises or sights in our environment. After hearing a sound or looking at an object repeatedly over a period of time, we eventually fail to react to it or see it in a fresh way.

> *Meditation is not to condition our minds but to free us,*
> *to liberate us from compulsive functioning*
> *or habitual emotional responses.*

A research study of electrical resistance of the skin showed a sharp change took place when the subject heard a loud click for the first time—an unconscious response not under voluntary control. But when repeated every five seconds, there was less response, until after the third or fourth click, none was evident.

However, when Zen masters were exposed to the same stimulus every five seconds for five minutes, they did not show the customary habituation but responded to the last click just as they did the first. Each experience was as if it were new. This simple experiment not only demonstrates the profound effects meditation can have upon our central nervous system (as demonstrated in many research experiments), but may have far-reaching implications. We do not want to become hardened to life but to stay more vitally alive.

Much recent psychological research has provided a basis for understanding how we create our own world, how we distort and misinform ourselves about what goes on around us, how our perceptions affect what we see, yet how it is indeed possible to reflect our environment to live in the present more completely.

We find one important example in our relationships with those we love. The degree to which we see our loved one as an object is the degree to which love seems to fade as we become more habituated to the presence of that person in our lives. Only as we relate to the loved one as much more than an object to possess, to comfort or stimulate or give to us, do we find a love that grows. Then love is new each day. Meditation, we now see, cleanses the windows of perception, and our personal world more closely matches reality. (Read Naranjo and Ornstein for more experiments in and implications of the results of meditation.[2])

Please recall the ultimate purpose of meditation is to clear the mind so the pure essence of the higher nature may be experienced. Our preparations, focus, concentration, and meditation set the stage for touching into the transcendental field. However, some paths to illumination have an emphasis beyond resting in the experience of pure being. For these, it is not enough to know the state of bliss. Bliss is merely experiencing the spiritual quality of our essence. But Christianity teaches we are to bring this higher state of reality into the machinations of the world, into our relationships with others, into our thoughts and feelings about ourselves, and ultimately into action to bring about moral and ethical change. So too does the practice of Agni Yoga, or "Living Ethics," as these teachings also are known.

As noted earlier, the Agni Yoga teachings were dictated by a member of the spiritual hierarchy known as Master Morya, or El Morya, to Helena Roerich, wife of Nicholas Roerich. The Roerichs were of aristocratic Russian backgrounds, yet avant-garde in their personal approaches to life. They embraced culture as the great tool of peace and unity for humankind.

Agni concepts, compatible with Christian backgrounds, speak of the near future as a time of human enlightenment as illumination is achieved by the peoples of the world. Agni Yoga provides ethical standards for humanity through focus upon purposeful themes. Imagine Agni as tongues of flame guiding humanity through purification to enlightenment.

In creation realize the happiness of life, and unto the desert turn thine eye. Comprehend the great gift of love to the One God. Try to unfold the power of insight, that you may perceive the future unity of [hu]mankind. The one salvation is to turn the spirit toward the light of Truth. The great gift of love lies in the one vision bestowed upon the fearless soul. Thou, who hast seen!

—Helena Roerich, *Leaves of Morya's Garden*

All modern-day spiritual paths concur: we must learn to translate our essence into the ways in which we work, play, love, eat, sleep, and create. Only then will the world be transformed into a true reflection of the wonder and perfection of its Source. While Agni Yoga is one example of a modern path that seeks to metamorphose its practitioners, Integral Yoga[3] and Solar Yoga, taught by Aurobindo and Master Aïvanhov, respectively, to name but two, also place the emphasis on transformation.

Bliss is experiencing the spiritual quality of our essence.

Throughout subsequent lessons, we will recommend ways to bring meditation experiences into daily living. Through meditation and disciplines of living, we can truly become soul-infused personalities. The goal of soul infusion is to allow the powers of the soul to express freely through the personality. This grants great freedom to the soul and is a significant step toward self-actualization. Naturally and inevitably, we will then extend this essence into all we see and touch and do. Our pure being will reflect our perfect nature in increasingly accurate ways.

In a continuing effort to accomplish this, we align ourselves harmoniously with the Plan, the divine evolutionary pattern for eventual universal at-one-ment. So, more than a personal clearing of our minds, meditation becomes part of our total commitment to a richer, more fulfilled life. Through meditation and conscious refocusing of our life patterns, we "let it begin with me."

As said in *The Science of Meditation,*

. . . a human being is a spiritual entity occupying a personality form. The personality itself is composed of four vehicles, or bodies: the mental, emotional, etheric and

Helpful Steps toward Successful Meditation

A quiet environment. Find a place of quiet so as to be uninterrupted for a time. Remember to disconnect the telephone. Choosing the same time and place daily reinforces our practice and strengthens associations that help us "shift gears."

A comfortable position. It is not necessary to have a particular posture, but it is important to be comfortable so you are not distracted by awareness of the body. A straight-backed chair is a good way to begin, but do not lean back. Hold your spine comfortably erect.

Focus upon a word, thought, or symbol. For the mind to be centered, it must have a point of reference. We use mandalas, words, symbols, or seed thoughts to accomplish this. A point of focus keeps the imagination from pulling us one way or another. Many teachings suggest, "Keep the name of God upon your lips always." As he was felled by an assassin, the last word Gandhi uttered was "Ram." "Om" or "Christ" may be words to use when beginning.

A receptive attitude. Be willing to present yourself for the experience and to be there. We need nothing elaborate to get started. Think of yourself as a willing chalice, ready to be filled. Now visualize a bright light shining down upon you from ten inches or so over your head. You will recall from lesson 1, we call this point of light the soulstar. Enjoy seeing (in your mind's eye), feeling (its warmth and love like the sun's rays), and being in this Presence. After a short time—I recommend sitting quietly in this relaxed, focused manner twenty minutes or so—you will gradually move your attention outward, having found a more positive state of mind, your body relaxed, and your spirits lifted.

dense physical. Meditation is concerned with the right use and control of these vehicles, their integration into a unified, coordinated whole and finally, the fusion of the integrated personality with the soul.

Each of the personality vehicles is the agent of a particular type of energy and experience, providing both a mechanism of perception and a means of expression. The *mind,* or mental body, distinguishes the true from the false, evaluates facts and weighs the opinions and ideas of others. The mind plans and decides; it is essentially a creative mechanism. The *emotional* body is that component of the personality which perceives and expresses feelings—love, hate, desire, longing, anger, or the scores of other emotions. The *etheric* body is the energy body, which interpenetrates dense physical matter and conditions it by the type and quality of energy flowing through the etheric channels. The etheric is the medium of contact and response with the ocean of energies in which we live. The *dense physical* vehicle functions largely as an automaton, responding to the thoughts and feelings which flow, as energies, through the etheric body, motivating physical activities.

Work in meditation is required to harmonise the thinking and feeling faculties, to coordinate and integrate the mental and emotional bodies into a coherent whole, evoking the flow of energy from the soul. With the mind, the emotional and physical bodies under the guidance of spiritual purpose, inner conflicts are resolved and the integrated personality becomes a pure vehicle of soul expression, a means of releasing greater light and love into the world of human affairs.

from the Alice A. Bailey materials
prepared by the Arcane School[4]

Passive meditation works to adjust personality to make it conscious of some higher point of awareness. Soul-infused personality means a coworking relationship between the soul and personality has been achieved. When the personality-made-ready (integration of the three lower bodies) has been accomplished, this prepared personality can be aligned with the soul. The more this interaction occurs, the sooner we will reach soul infusion.

Some inner action must assist in giving credence to the veiled self. We integrate will, heart, and mind through daily experience. We overcome the disharmony of our physical nature, our emotions, and our restless, scanning mind as they struggle among themselves. At an immature stage we sabotage our heart's desire by willfulness or lack of will; later we find our heart pulls toward emotionalism even as our mind knows what path is wisest.

As we integrate the lessons learned, personality learns to move gracefully to an objective position, where "witness consciousness" is evolving. This blending of energies into a smooth, working unit is truly allowing an eye, High Self, to form that is empowered to reflect to personality the wisdom it has gathered through its historical journey. As this mechanism is integrated into a refined whole, we enhance sensitivity and we acquire what is known as an integrated personality or personality made-ready. This is a great goal for the basic self, just as soul infusion is the great goal of personality.

The Christ's message of love has had to wait a long time for fruition. Perhaps we received too great a vision for the humanity of the Piscean age.

Our three vehicles will struggle for control. Each has its own agenda. These pulls are instinctual (physical), desirous (emotional), and illusionary (mental). Each "body" has to be fed, cleansed, and exercised for soul infusion to be realized. That is to say, each level has to be energized (fed) in order to unfold or develop whatever level of excellence it can possibly attain. Each must be purified (cleansed) of false or outgrown efforts and disciplined (exercised) so we can do, or not do, as discernment dictates. As all of this is experienced, we advance on the Path of Initiation.

The message to love others is an authentic and transcendent revelation for the student of Esoteric Christianity. The coming of the Christ anchored the principle of love for the planet. This new principle was to affect the consciousness of all humanity. Thus we see universality also woven into the Christian message. Esoteric Christianity seeks to both integrate and communicate this.

The disciples kept the message alive, and the message was spread throughout the world over many generations as the word of Christ. However, we also see that few followers have been able to live the message. Christ's words seem to have lain like seeds under the soil, waiting for humanity to mature sufficiently to undertake such a work. As we enter the Aquarian age, recall Master Jesus's message as he prepared to enter Jerusalem and told his people to follow the man carrying the jug on his shoulder to an upper room prepared for them (Mark 14.13,14). Some believe this suggests the man carrying the jug is the water bearer, Aquarius, and that only now can humanity be led to the higher consciousness for which it is ready.

This thought correlates with other arcane spiritual teachings. Only now has enough mind-stuff been assimilated for humanity to use it consciously and for good. We continue building the ever-forming mental vehicle. As noted earlier, first humanity developed the reptilian brain; then it evolved the mammalian brain. Most recently, we have had the task of developing the neocortex. We are rapidly discovering many specific abilities of right and left hemispheres and how they integrate. While we still have a great deal to learn, enough has been proven for us to realize we have not mastered our potential. As we wisely use the decision-making process of the left hemisphere and the relationship-remembrance of the right hemisphere, they synthesize their capabilities, and we learn discernment and discrimination. We discover our intuitive self which links us to higher knowledge or revelation.

The Christ's message of love has had to wait a long time for fruition. Perhaps we received too great a vision for the humanity of the Piscean age. Perhaps the seed planted in the unconscious of humanity has matured and it will now surface and bear fruit. Many see it this way.

It seems we are awakening in a new way to the great goal of life, and new techniques are emerging to help us reach that goal. Agni, the modern technique for self-directed individuals, is a fervent path for helping aspirants evolve as they listen to wise mentors and their own inner teacher, and are inspired and supported by those traveling the path with them. Remember, the Agni way serves without conflict as a path of ethics for the non-religious and religious alike. Later, we will draw upon Agni themes for seed thoughts, thus assuring ourselves of an ecumenical perspective with respect for all paths.

Preparation for Meditation Training

As we continue to provide suggestions for more effective meditation, you will see several ways to proceed to achieve the same thing. These procedures have helped many others. To begin with, use a single method, such as relaxation, for two or more weeks to give it a reasonable trial. All types of activities facilitate meditation: relaxation, centering, lifestyle changes, and others still to be included. If your meditations are not satisfying from time to time, return to earlier lessons for review.

Another Centering Procedure

In previous lessons we described a breathing exercise designed to promote rest and serenity. Here is another with subtle but powerful effects. Remember to treat all breathing exercises with caution and respect.

Alternate nostril breathing is an ancient and popular yoga procedure. Roy Eugene Davis,[5] a teacher initiated into Kriya Yoga by Paramahansa Yogananda, advocates its use just before beginning to meditate as a means of harmonizing the flow of vital forces, calming the mind, cleansing the nervous system, and relieving anxiety. When we are so stressed or distraught we find it difficult to meditate or even to function adequately, this technique can restore a significant degree of serenity and balance.

As you sit comfortably erect, hold the right nostril closed with your thumb, and inhale easily through the left nostril. Take in a complete breath, but do not strain. Hold it briefly, then close the left nostril with your finger, and exhale through the right. Then inhale through the right nostril, hold it a moment, and exhale through the left. This is one complete cycle. Repeat seven to ten times, and then rest from the technique. If you need to repeat, wait at least half an hour before doing so. Do not do more than two cycles in a series.

With this technique, it is best to breathe in and out fairly slowly and to keep the inhalations and exhalations about the same length of time. Fill the lower and then the upper lungs, but do not work hard at it. One variation is to hold the breath for a longer period and to pause between breaths. This process is similar to the rhythmic breathing in lesson 2, but the subtle effects involving control of vital forces are quite different because of breathing through alternate nostrils.

If you have not used this procedure before, try it gently for a week or two. Many who have done so even intermittently through the years find it beneficial in numerous ways. The exercise can be calming when you are nervous, depressed, or agitated, but should not be overdone at any one time.

Daily Cleansing

Many procedures exist for purification of the body as a preparation for meditation.[6] We may take on so many practices, the total routine becomes too time-consuming and burdensome. It is preferable to select a few procedures that fit easily into our routine.

Daily bathing is important. It removes accumulated dirt, oils, and dead skin cells. If your situation does not always permit this, take a symbolic shower. Visualize yourself standing in a shower of light which streams down over the body, cleansing the aura of all impurities. Remember, the skin is an organ of elimination, and the adage, "Cleanliness is next to godliness," is ancient.

Diego de Lando, a friar writing in the 16th century about the Maya as their culture was being decimated, commented on their cleanliness and how their religion emphasized bathing at least once a day. The Spaniards of that time, unfamiliar with temple traditions, were shocked. Similarly, the Hindu tradition considers it absolutely necessary to bathe the physical body daily—in some schools of thought, both morning and evening.

While brushing your teeth, gently clean the gums and tongue. A quick cleansing of the mouth upon rising is done by holding water in the mouth while you run your tongue over your gums, cheeks, teeth, and soft palate. Release the water into the washbowl, and stick your tongue out as far as possible; as you pull it back into the mouth, scrape the surface with your upper teeth. This not only cleans the tongue but encourages clearing mucus from the throat. Or very gently use your toothbrush on your tongue and inside your mouth.

After cleansing the mouth, drink half a glass of water with lemon juice as a way to stimulate cleansing the internal organs. All this takes only a few moments and prepares us to approach meditation in a condition most receptive to the flow of higher vital energies. These techniques are highly recommended in the Hindu *Kriya Yoga approach, as well as many others.

Certain basic truths given to disciples over the ages were intended primarily for the purification of personality. Training has been disseminated through all traditions to help the physical and emotional natures sensitize to the touch of consciousness. While none of this is true esoteric teaching, it corresponds with rules of probationer training and begins transformation of the aspirant. The form or manner of lifestyle is upgraded so that the desired and appreciated touch of spirit is most readily felt. Devotion to a particular path has been a most successful tool for the candidate for probationary training. We recall the popular Twelve-Step Program and its many variations as the probationary path supplying the necessary discipline to re-form lifestyles. Form is important in the early stages of initiation.

Another Position for Meditation

If you have not found a comfortable way to sit with the spine erect for extended periods, consider the use of a zen bench. This low, sloping bench allows you to assume the position of sitting on the calves of your legs, without weight on your feet and legs and without bending the knees uncomfortably. It holds the body erect with the diaphragm open and spine straight. It is actually a variation of kneeling, with the weight resting on the knees and on the small, sloping seat above the calves. (Be sure you take your shoes off.)

If you should tire, relax forward for a minute or two, then return to a sitting posture. After a bit of practice, the muscles needed to hold you upright will strengthen. This posture leaves the body free to function as an antenna, the stirring current will act upon the spiritual centers, and the energy can move freely without restriction. If knees have been a problem, be careful with the zen bench. Knees and feet do stretch and relax, but go carefully, sitting in posture for brief periods until you are comfortable for a longer time. Do not force your body; give it time to adjust. Many feel the zen bench enhances their meditation. Building plans are detailed below for your information. Benches are available from our center and many other metaphysical centers or bookstores.

Figure 13. Detail of Zen Bench.

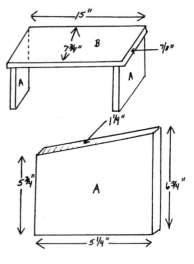

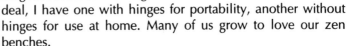

The zen bench, a simple structure composed of three pieces of wood, is made even more comfortable by padding the seat with foam and covering it with a fabric of your choice. The cross seat can be measured to your specifications. The thicknesses of the wood may vary from the above measurements, as well as the height of the legs. The key to comfort is the front and back measurements: the back side of the end piece should measure one inch higher than the front.

The three pieces of wood may be glued or nailed together; for easy travel, the legs can be hinged. Because I travel a great deal, I have one with hinges for portability, another without hinges for use at home. Many of us grow to love our zen benches.

Energy follows thought is an axiom well known to spiritual students. As we begin to understand meditation, it is helpful to remember we are focusing our attention at a mental level, either following the guiding thoughts of another, listening to a meditation tape, or working with a seed thought. The energy that follows thought is now flowing into the *mental body, as it is called in *spiritual science. Think of this as energizing to the mind, expanding and stimulating new levels, creating the new mental potentials promised to humanity in John 14.12: *He who believes in me shall do the works which I do; and even greater than these things he shall do.*

As mind expands, it first creates what we know as "abstract mind." This vast range of thought postulates rather than rationalizes. It dances and leaps in response to concepts; it seeks to experience oneness and to comprehend how the mysteries of life are reconciled. Those of this bent—philosophers and mystics—find satisfying links between the rational and the divine.

Guided meditation with its open moments allows High Self to give its gifts to the practitioner. In the guided-meditation work, spaces occur when what is held in the ball of knowledge (High Self) may be presented to personality for its consideration. Remember, personality finds its guide in the High Self, and soul purpose is found at a higher level. Soul purpose, hidden at the soul level, is generally not revealed until nearer soul infusion.

As we come upon new concepts, they are quite likely to challenge our old comfortable ideas and create a bit of a struggle. If something does not feel right, just put it on an imaginary shelf. From time to time, take it down and look at it. You can put it back on the shelf or choose to allow it to become a tool for your personal use. This is right use of will and, as we are able to comprehend more, we will need a greater variety of ways with which to view life.

This realization will be of great value as we meet new metaphysical *(meta* = "beyond") beliefs from world religions other than those of our personal background. Because we live in an era of breakthroughs, we will in all likelihood be challenged time and again with new, seemingly preposterous ideas. Then, just recall your bookshelf!

Assignment

Two exercises follow. The first is to give your imagination opportunity to express in a disciplined way. We are learning to use the image-making mechanism. These continue to be passive meditations and hasten the awakening of inner sensitivity. Do each of these several times and write down the results for your tutor. Let us know of your sense of radiating beauty and your sense of joining with others to lift all humanity to higher consciousness.

EXERCISE: BE A FLOWER
Purpose: To gift the beauty of self to the outer world

Enjoy the beautiful scenery of thoughts in the invisible, intangible kingdom within you.
—Paramahansa Yogananda

1. Begin to relax with several natural breaths; add singing, chanting, or music for a few minutes.

2. Become still and continue to relax. Close your eyes and turn your attention inward. Spend a few minutes relaxing your body into a comfortable position with spine erect, shoulders relaxed, feet flat on the floor—or on your zen bench.

3. Become aware of a light over your head, your soulstar. You are resting in the light of the soul.

4. Draw the soulstar energy to your heart. Magnify your positive feelings of caring. Allow this energy to flow. Feel it move through your emotional nature—clearing, cleansing, and nurturing. Consciously bless the body. Feel a deep appreciation for it. Let this positive energy, caring and nurturing, flow through the emotional nature and the body, healing past hurts, forgiving, and releasing all negativity. Fill yourself with the positive energy of the soulstar, and radiate that light into the space around you.

5. Before proceeding, rest in this energy for a brief time.

6. Using the rule of acting "as if" now, perceive yourself as a flower blooming, as you experience the sun shining upon you. Absorb the light, feel its warmth and energy flowing to you.

7. When you are nourished by this warm energy you have contacted, sensing your own aura filled with the energy you are receiving, radiate the beauty—as the flower that you are—to the world about you, both as a service and as an expression of gratitude for that which you have received. Emanate the energy from your soulstar. See beauty and positive energy flowing through you, out into the room, to the environment, to the world.

8. Be gentle with yourself. Take a nice long breath as you prepare to return your attention to the world about you. Remember your closing gesture, and conclude this work by speaking the sacred tone, *Om,* aloud three times with appreciation.

MEDITATION EXERCISE:
HUMANITY INVOKES HIGH CONSCIOUSNESS
Purpose: To assist humanity in knowing its higher nature

The oldest wisdom in the world tells us we can consciously unite with the divine whilst in the body; for this, man is really born. If he misses his destiny, nature is not in a hurry. She will catch him up someday and compel him to fulfill her secret purpose.

—Rhada Krishnan

Universally a quickening of the spirit is taking place. The Christ light, as known to Christians, is flooding the planet, seeking receptive souls through which to do its work in the world. In meditation we would catch that light (inspiration), allow love (Lots Of Vital Energy) to flow, and partake of that spiritual power (will). We would experience the Divine awakened.

1. Use preparatory chanting or background music. It is best to learn some simple chants. If you have difficulty with this, let us know; we have quite a number on paper and on tape. You may chant along with the tape, mindful of the benefits to the reptilian level of the brain—important.

2. Become still, eyes closed. Use your opening gesture, and draw the light of the soulstar down from over your head (from about ten inches above).

3. Relax the body; be comfortable. Be as relaxed and centered as possible. When you note tension or tiredness in the body, lean forward, rest a minute or two, and then return to your posture. Do not be concerned because, with practice, your body will strengthen where needed. Remain relaxed and centered. Focus on the sense of the light flowing to you.

4. Allow the energy of the light to penetrate deep into your being. Observe the light, love, and power of the soulstar pouring into you. Know this essence is blessing and transforming you, filling you with new energy with which to meet life.

5. As the Presence seems to fade, feel it take residence more securely within your being. The mind seems empowered. The heart is stimulated, open, receptive to new experience, to caring sensitivity. Now speak The Great Invocation:

> *From the point of Light within the Mind of God*
> *Let light stream forth into the minds of men.*
> *Let Light descend on Earth.*

Now visualize yourself receiving the light and radiating it into the world. At the conclusion of each spoken segment, think to yourself, "through me."

> *From the point of Love within the Heart of God*
> *Let love stream forth into the hearts of men.*
> *May Christ return to Earth. ("through me")*

See an outpouring surge of Love flowing forth to humanity and the Christ consciousness returning to Earth in and through the many who offer themselves.

> *From the center where the Will of God is known*
> *Let purpose guide the little wills of men—*
> *The purpose which the Masters know and serve.*
> *("through me")*

See yourself standing strong, in place as a world server committed and ready, willing to do your part, eager to fulfill your purpose.

> *From the center which we call the race of men*
> *Let the Plan of Love and Light work out*
> *And may it seal the door where evil dwells. ("with my help")*

See yourself standing shoulder to shoulder with other disciples, forming a line of light, holding back and neutralizing the miasma—the negativity humanity has created on both the physical and the astral planes.

Let Light and Love and Power restore the Plan on Earth.

6. Now, together, awakened to the light and love and power of the higher nature and the resources available to us, we speak the sacred tone, the *Om,* three times, consciously sending the energy of the true Self to bless our world, to heal and to help, thinking the command, "Go and do a Holy Work."

Om   Om   Om

7. Now, as we are aligned to the energy of light and love and spiritual power, we return to the world about us, recharged, restored. Aware of the light within, we serve the Plan we perceive, doing well this work, that greater work may be revealed.

8. To close, speak aloud: Amen, or Shanti, or your preferred power word, followed by the closing gesture you have selected. Be gentle with yourself as you refocus on the outer world once again.

Power Words

Amen — So be it, or I affirm it is so.
Shanti— Peace, like the peace that passes understanding.
Shalom — The peace of the inner reality.
Mir — Peace, in Russian.
Ho — The Native American "I affirm it is so."

We Are the Technology

For as the rain and the snow come down from heaven, and
returns not thither, but waters the earth and makes it bring forth
and sprout and gives seed to the sower and bread to the eater;
so shall my word be that goes forth out of my mouth; it shall not
return to me void, but it shall do what I please and
it shall accomplish that for which I sent it.

Isaiah 55.10,11

Although we will outline several meditation procedures, it will be useful to emphasize certain points in the process to prevent their getting lost in the content of the lessons.

As we have learned, proper use of awareness, discipline, study, and insight is exercised to hold the mind clear and focused as the emotional nature is stimulated, to a greater or lesser degree, to help us penetrate higher realms, the Cloud of Knowable Things. Most of us need some instruction in order to understand how sensitive the human make-up is to vibrations. The sensing mechanism is designed to alert us to influences not recognizable by our rational mind. We either feel good about something or we do not. It has little to do with evaluation, although that is our customary approach. We usually attempt to rationalize why we feel the way we do. In meditation work we use this sensitivity to purify our nature of distortions and prepare for a higher reality.

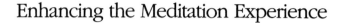

Enhancing the Meditation Experience

Music is a wonderful tool to prepare us for meditation. Both East and West use chanting in some form; Native American chants are growing in popularity. Choose a chant of one or two lines, such as "Spirit of the Living God" or "Surely the Presence of the Lord Is in This Place," to begin your meditation. We can acquaint you with a variety of chants; many of our seminarians use a tape of songs and chants we recorded, *LCCC Sings.*[1]

As you read a page or two of devotional material, adopt a contemplative attitude, and allow the thoughts that arise to settle deep within. Close your eyes, and visualize a point of clear white light ten inches or so over your head. Focus upon this vibrating light, the soulstar, and allow it to expand its radiance, remaining clear and bright. Image the light, feel the light, experience the light.

Begin your relaxation with a series of gentle breaths, nice and long, relaxing the body with each one. Follow the breath in and out, giving the mental suggestion, "Relax, let go. Be in peace."

Saraydarian sees meditation as answering the call of our innermost essence, a plea for release, freedom, and liberation. We all encounter hindrances on the Path, but "the disciple is not paralyzed by obstacles; he is inflamed more and more with a continuous inner radiance. He even enjoys obstacles because he grows through them."[2]

When we consciously seek to express love, freedom, beauty, and joy in our day-to-day activity, we evoke what we in the Christian tradition have come to know as *grace.* This potent, elusive, and hard-to-understand outpouring blesses us and expands our consciousness. Grace results in a spiritual, transforming state—mind, body, or experience.

Love, freedom, beauty, and joy bring grace into our lives, releasing us from restriction. A simple idea for invoking grace is to practice these in word and action: love, freedom, beauty, and joy, the real building blocks. Grace is the resulting shift in awareness, breaking through our limitations and liberating us. This may relate to a state of mind or a condition existing in the physical, such as healing. Nevertheless, the nature of grace is to deliver us into a new state.

To gain grace we focus upon invoking the love which moves Lots Of Vital Energy through the opened heart center. We affirm freedom to become all we are meant to be. We realize beauty feeds the soul. And we seek the joy that comes as we achieve contact with the soul in all its uniqueness. While happiness comes and goes and relates to the outer state of things, joy has to do with a touch of soul, or samadhi. Joy sustains us whether the events of life are good or challenging, a state of mind that results from inner contact.

Although authors may use different language, they essentially agree that meditation is necessary to develop spiritually. Meditative techniques may be used for legitimate practical benefits, but we must go beyond this if we wish to experience freedom, self-realization, illumination, or soul infusion. In this work we assume you are dedicated to attaining the fullest and highest level of spiritual development possible in this lifetime.

> Perhaps the great disaster of human history is one that happened to or within religion: that is, the conceptual division between the holy and the world, the excerpting of the Creator from the creation.
> —Wendell Berry, *A Continuous Harmony*

It helps to remember "religious" and "spiritual" are not synonymous. *Religion* is a formal, defined approach to realignment with God through the directives of a particular tradition. *Spirituality* frees the spirit of the self-within to express more clearly. Religions are based upon the teachings, the ways and means by which divinity was realized by a wayshower. Those witnessing the transformative experience sought to do so as well. They adopted, debated, and decided what seemed to play a part in the changes they had witnessed, and they formulated "rules" to guide the development of those upon that path.

The emergence of spirituality, the natural state of the mature soul, is similar to what occurs when someone grows wise through experience. At opportune moments, our choices allow the spirit to merge more vigorously into personality. As it is empowered, this spirit-essence of self transforms personality gradually to cooperate with and then to serve the soul. Spirituality allows the essence of the real Self to be revealed. The science of expressing our true nature in the midst of personality's domain is "spirituality." We comprehend this in those brief moments of great clarity.

Thus, we have begun systematic self-exploration to enrich our meditation and our lives. The process, designed to explore meditation while assisting in clearing mental and emotional barriers, becomes much more than mere inner activity; it has an increased direct and indirect influence upon living more deeply, more fully, and more joyously.

Soul infusion is the goal of human consciousness at this evolutionary stage. Meditation techniques are designed to transform a particular level of mind. At the same time, as we individually expand in consciousness, we are also building the group mind. Advanced meditation techniques seek to contact the soul and affect our personality. As these two interact, personality adjusts to the soul time and again. And as we work on ourselves, corresponding changes occur in the group mind. Much more is accomplished than we readily recognize.

Passive meditation provides us with ways to engage in a variety of exercises to gain new awareness. It helps us trigger hidden challenges to assist the growth of our personality. The leader invokes our cooperation and takes us into guided fantasy, supplying brief sketches of images. Our own creative self becomes involved and supplies details from its resources. Our subtle senses respond with symbolic implications, and soon we gain an insight or better understanding of the hidden part of our nature and what it knows.

A leader of guided meditations has the task of directing the process. At the outset, an environment of trust should be established. No one should participate in an altered-state-of-consciousness exercise feeling suspicion, fear, or great inner resistance. Mere lack of knowledge or experience is not a reason to fear participation, but lack of trust of either the other participants, the leader, or the place is ample reason for abstaining.

The leader consciously chooses a meditation scenario that leads toward an articulated goal. The goal needs to be any healthy, purposeful state of consciousness. The leader focuses the intent of the meditation work. The participant(s) follows, with the guide leaving certain open "spaces" for the participant's image-maker to supply ideas, symbols, messages, and actions. In this way the High Self is given room to insert pertinent pieces, even though the symbolic adventure is being shaped by an outer leader. A trained observer can learn much about the development and inner life of another through such activity.

Similarly, individuals may gather for guided meditations as a means to unify the levels of consciousness of a group in order to focus upon an intent and, linked together, have a greater impact in the area of their service. Joining with others in such alliances is highly effective in attracting particular energies and redirecting them in a desired way.

We do the following and many other unique works in meditation:
- we direct healing energies;
- we gather new information;
- we reinforce the grids of the planet;
- we serve humanity and the younger kingdoms; and
- we affirm right relationship to one another and our coworkers.

Selected purposes are known as specific-work meditations. While many are well known, I will include directions for those given. We are to discover that we are able to employ our spiritual senses for many objectives. We receive messages from a teacher or friend in spirit. We invoke various energies or qualities to ourselves. We link to others. We surround ourselves or others with protective influences. We perform new moon and full moon meditations to contact celestial influences. And remember, we are not limited to these few.

Important: Details discovered in exercises such as the following are personal and should be treated as private, not shared unless or until you choose. No one should attempt to pry meditation experiences, insights, or realizations from another. Sharing needs to be voluntary, with a mentor or in a class situation. Again, respect must be accorded to information gained in such a way. Share with tutors or others only in a way you have deliberately chosen.

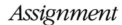

Assignment

Practice each of the following exercises several times. According to your personal experience, you will choose the next step. If you have already done a great deal of passive meditation, you are ready to proceed to active meditation techniques. If not, it is best to gain experience with guided meditations or what we call passive work. If you have had little past experience in this area, repeat these exercises a number of times before advancing to the next lesson.

Exercise: Full Moon Meditation
Purpose: To become aligned with celestial influences

The Working Hypothesis: A coworking relationship between the sun and moon helps humanity come to fuller consciousness. The sun (solar) influence invites us to *know* ourselves, our personal traits, and the tools we have—our talents for expressing the rich facets of our spiritual self. While the sun challenges us to work in a conscious way, the moon (lunar) influence ebbs and flows, swells and swirls, tosses and turns us every which way to keep us unconsciously moving forward—for ourselves and for the whole.

In meditations at the time of full moon, we consciously explore and stimulate our nature at each level: physical behaviors, stamina, habits for health and vitality; emotional temperament and stability; mental inclinations and capabilities. We use the light of the soul, our high consciousness, to study ourselves while the solar light is high and the subconscious nature is both stirred and more available to us.

Engaging this human openness, the hierarchy of the empowered constellation pours forth blessings to help initiates comprehend and advance in building the desired nature. With the growth of each individual, the group and humanity as a whole also progress. While the energy is provided generously each full moon, a relatively small number of aspirants are trained to assist humanity in anchoring its treasures. However, interest is growing as respect for the divine feminine increases.

Moon festivals, such as full moon and new moon rituals, are celebrated as times when the feminine nature that expresses through the subconscious is empowered to reveal more of the hidden nature. Our connection to the Plan is held at this level, out of sight for most. Each moon festival, the sensitive feminine nature is contacted to encourage that which is hidden to gently be made known.

Special dedications for seed-thought work often are conducted on the contact day, three days prior to, and three days following each full moon. Consider adding these thoughts to your meditations on these special days.

Suggestions to learn to work with nature in her cycles are made for those who embrace the concept of meditation as valid and for those who feel ready to learn about the stimulating influences provided humanity through astrological energies. The full moon period is the time of strongest energy bombardment during each regular cyclic period.

Full moon meditations certainly lend themselves to movement, color, and sound effect or emphasis. With our natures so sensitive at this time, great advantages will accrue by adding these influences of the senses. However, to be positive and beneficial, the work must be done in a sensitive manner and with special regard to selections of dance, music, and color.

For a guide to sun sign information, full moon techniques, and other celebrations of a celestial nature, I would refer you to *The Book of Rituals,* published in 1990.[3] Here you will find full moon meditations for each sun sign, as well as rituals and meditations for other annual celebrations.

EXERCISE: CONTACTING THE INNER CHILD
Purpose: An aid to discover the needs of the basic
nature and insights into its healing.

Begin by moving into a deeply relaxed state.

You are walking down a hallway. At the end of the hallway, you come to a door. The door is locked, but a key is in the keyhole. You turn the key and slowly open the door. Inside this room is a child. The child is you. Describe the room. What do you see? Light or darkness? What things are in the room? What colors? How is the child dressed? etc.

Speak softly to the child. The child is hurt. How is it hurt? What can you do to help it? It may take some time to gain its trust. Continue to coax and speak softly and lovingly to the child until you are permitted to touch it, hold it, caress it, show it the love it deserves. You comfort it and tell it everything will be all right.

Comfort the child for a time. Soothe it. Let the child know it can trust you. Take it out of the room and back into the hallway. Carry it or lead it down the hallway to another door. This door is also locked, but again the key is in the keyhole. Unlock the door, and look inside, and let the child see also. This is the perfect room for your child. Describe it. What color are the walls? There is an access to the outdoors. Look at all the things in the room. What is there for this child? Everything in this room is for its benefit or pleasure. Introduce the child to its new surroundings. Give the child a bath, and dress it in new clothes or pajamas. Then continue to hold it and love it and soothe it.

You may leave the child in its new room, but you leave the door open and explain to the child that it may call you or leave the room anytime it wishes, to go to the kitchen, or the bathroom, or anywhere else. If it calls, you will come. Also explain that you will spend some time with it every day. Then, follow through on this promise by spending a few minutes each morning getting in touch with the child and finding out its needs for the day.

Leave the child only when it has reached the point at which it is content to stay in the room and be alone. If it wants to come with you when you leave, that's all right too. After all, this child is a part of you and certainly nothing to be ashamed of or hidden away. It is now your responsibility as an adult to nurture, protect, and care for this child. It deserves the very best from you in all areas of life.

Be gentle with your child as you return outward. Allow the child to live in your life. Take a deep breath. When you are ready, open your eyes, and use your closing gesture.

EXERCISE: MEDITATION FOR EXPERIENCING YOUR DEATH
Purpose: To assist us in living more consciously

In a quiet and meditative mood, as detached as possible, we begin to visualize the death we each await. As we create our death, we make it as pleasant and comfortable as possible for all those people we wish to be present. We plan details which suit us, for since we write the script, we can do it our own way. When we are seriously ill, we may be eager to create the ending of this stage of life and prepare for the beginning of the new.

Now visualize your physical body, the inner spirit withdrawn, family members reacting to the news of your death, friends helpful and tearful. Be conscious of unfinished matters that would fall upon others, perhaps the disposal of property and possessions. At the end of your particular life, what else would be left undone?

If you feel strong resistance to these thoughts, know this is perfectly natural. Most of us avoid this kind of thinking because it is unpleasant and requires a great deal of work. In this relaxed, detached awareness, unlock your inner thoughts.

Do you need to speak a kind word to another? Do you need to forgive someone or to release another from a debt? Who really cares for you that you have failed to recognize? Would you like to leave something to someone you haven't thought about before?

Do you see the wisdom in such forethought? I hope so. I know a number of people who are trying to think in this manner so they can leave this life peacefully, with others well aware of their love, remembered in a happy, comforting way.

With this kind of exercise, it is important to make notes and to consider how to act upon the impressions you receive. This exercise is to stimulate your inner nature, to remind you to put your life in order, and to acknowledge others who love and care about you. One lady I know wrote Christmas cards to her friends, including a "last" note. She wanted to say she cared one more time, and this was the way she did it—leaving the cards to be mailed the Christmas following her death.

This exercise is meaningful to everyone for the awareness it brings of the hole left in our lives when close ones depart. Think of a drill corps with one member dropping out and the adjustment required by the rest to close ranks. All of us touch more lives than we know. Death is especially relevant in this example, but many other major life changes result in similar experiences. Just think of the loneliness we feel when a near and dear family moves to another residence or city. Unwanted or unexpected change is painful.

With this imagery we become more aware of our interlocking ties. We honor them with new respect because of this meditation effort. We dedicate ourselves to keeping more in touch and to living more in the present from now on.

EXERCISE: PURIFICATION USING THE LIGHT OF THE SOUL
Purpose: To cleanse our subtle bodies of obstructions

Again, imagine your aura as an eggshell filling with the energy emanating from the soulstar and stepped down as the same love you contact through your heart. Bring this positive, radiant energy to swirl about you, over your head and body and beneath your knees and feet, clearing and cleansing your personal space of all negativity, old attitudes you no longer need. Even personal habits you are ready to release will be dissolved in this light of the soul. Hold the light, bright all about you, for a few moments, invoking the purifying power of the soul to work in and through your life and energy field.

Next, allow yourself to release a fine mist of ash, representing all that has been burned away in the purification work. See the ash falling beneath you, going deep into the heart of the Earth, blessing the Earth to bring forth new growth.

Create an affirmation to attest to this purification, such as:

In the light of the Soul I am cleansed and purified of old ideas, attitudes, and false beliefs that obscure the light.

In the light of the Soul, I am purified and renewed on the emotional level, that where there is need for healing, I am healed. Love and positive energy now flow freely through my entire emotional nature.

> *I invoke the light of the Soul to act upon my personal life and physical habits; may all those activities that hinder the Soul in its expression be burned away, cleansed, and released.*
>
> *I rejoice in purification and renewal. I give thanks for the action of my Soul in my daily life. Amen.*

EXERCISE:

MEDITATION FOR THE UNITED STATES GOVERNMENT[4]

Purpose: To align our government to the higher plane

Sound the Om three times, aligning the physical, emotional, and mental bodies with the Soul, the indwelling divinity.

As the Soul, see yourself as part of a network of light, pulsating and circulating between and among all individuals and groups around the United States and the world, working to build the new civilization of light and love, aligned with divine will.

Align with those great teachers, saints, and Masters of all religions who guide human evolution.

See the White House, and within it see the President and the Vice President, guided and protected by the great spiritual Masters, encompassed in a transparent shield of light of divine protection, a sphere of light which will allow them to accomplish their mission, free from harm and aligned with divine will for the United States. See our President and Vice President and all people in the administration working for the highest good of all peoples on Earth, in accord with divine will.

See an aura of light, guidance, and protection around the Congress and the people serving there. See a channel of light and cooperation flowing between the President and the Vice President and the leaders of Congress from both parties. See them working together cooperatively and wisely for the highest good of all people to pass legislation that will uplift and empower people everywhere to take action to solve their problems.

See light and wisdom flowing into the Supreme Court, inspiring decisions that uphold human laws aligned with higher spiritual law.

See light flowing in a triangle between these three branches of government, circulating around the three points of the triangle—the White House, the Congress, and the Supreme Court—and infused with the all-seeing eye from the pyramid on the Great Seal,[5] radiating light throughout the United States and the planet.

Close with the following Mantram of Unification[6] (or whatever prayer, or mantra from your practice you prefer).

All souls are one, and I am one with them.
I seek to love, not hate.
I seek to serve, and not exact due service.
I seek to heal, not hurt.

Let pain bring due reward of light and love.
Let the soul control the outer form,
And life, and all events,
And bring to light the love
That underlies the happenings of the time.

Let vision come, and insight.
Let the future stand revealed.
Let inner union demonstrate
And outer cleavages be gone.
Let love prevail.
Let all love.
Om   Om   Om

EXERCISE: A MEDITATION FOR HEALING
Purpose: We learn to assist others

Three steps to a healing experience.

First, we prepare ourselves.

Please close your eyes, and relax. Take a deep breath, and let us shift our attention to the source of light over our heads and invoke that light, love, and power as we prepare to serve as healing channels.

Bring the energy to the heart. Allow yourself to begin to think, "I care, I care." Feel the great outpouring of love of which you are capable. See your personality becoming increasingly attuned to your Lord, Master, Teacher—with whomever you are attuned.

Second, we direct the energy to flow to the one held in healing hope. "I now invoke the healing energy to flow to me and through me. As I seek to serve as a healing channel, may the healing forces of life flow to those I hold in thought. I direct the healing energy to ___(name)___, to bless and to flow to his/her high consciousness to aid this life and to bring forward right action in this body and in life experiences. May the healing energy flow." See the person, and continue to send energy for a few minutes.

Third, we give thanks for the opportunity to serve in this way. Closing: I give thanks for this opportunity to serve as a healing channel, for the blessings of my life, and for the new awareness that guides me on my way.   Amen.

Now speak the following:

Invocation for Healing
May the Great White Light of healing
be received by these souls in need.
May they be placed in the hands
of the Great Masters who heal.
May they be surrounded by God's Light,
and may we do our work in being
pure instruments toward this goal.   Amen.

Sound the *Om* aloud and release your focus. Take a breath. Begin to readjust to the feeling of the body. Again, a breath, and your closing gesture.

EXERCISE: BECOME A PLANETARY WORKER
Purpose: A meditation to bless the Earth

Now, let us think about the essence of spirit and matter which is our human nature. Their emanations stimulate us to perceive the beauty of balance and harmony in life. The power of spirit lifts and inspires; the power of matter introduces us to the peaceful, balanced energy we call the Laws of Nature. As these earthly influences reveal themselves to us, we quite naturally want to slow down, rest, and become comfortable in our bodies and in our world. As we awaken to our spiritual nature, we begin to realize we have potential to create harmony. As spiritually awakened ones, we are empowered to bring to Earth the beauty of higher worlds. We begin to know it is possible to transform our world into a garden of beauty and peace. We recognize the creative spirit housed within, and we invoke it to guide us in our work in the world.

Take a deep breath, and feel the peace flow through your body and your being. The wisdom of divinity bathes you. Feel love in your heart: love for life; love for self; love for others, and think, "I care." Feel love pulsating within you and through you, love for life around you, life within you, known and unknown. Feel that sense of caring blend with your sense of knowing.

Again, a breath. Feel your heart and mind—two streams of consciousness—merging. Feel yourself becoming compassionate, wise, and caring. Filled with the wisdom of higher consciousness, you dare to love, to be gentle but strong, caring but clear, a wise one. Know you are both spirit and matter, balancing the dualities of your human nature.

Know you are wise and sure, blessed by the energy of beauty, right-thought, and right-love. Inspired by the outpouring of high consciousness, you are aware of the self-within that receives wisdom and responds. You are awakened to perceive and realize through your channels of inner-knowing, and you rest in that awareness.

Now sit quietly, attuning your mind to Higher Mind. Focus your attention upon an image of the planet, creating it in your mind. Invoke celestial forces to assist humanity as it awakens to its divine nature. See the planet calming, clearing, and healing. Awakened ones attune their nature to the Creator and invoke creative power to reconstruct a life of goodness and beauty for humanity and all kingdoms.

Now, again, allow the bright light of wisdom to radiate from your head. Relax, feel the focused thought energy you have been using shine about your head like a halo of light. Expand this radiance to fill the space about you. Let it bless, touch, embrace, and encourage all that is in this space with you. Share the energy of your meditation with the world about you. See yourself anchoring the light of high consciousness in your life, in your home, and in your activity of healing and hope.

You are peaceful now. Become receptive, and welcome the light and love others bestow. Even as you have shared, now draw the blessings of other workers to you, and see yourself linked to the light workers of planetary life. Take a breath, and ground those incoming energies to your own being.

Now see the planet encircled with a wondrous grid of light; all around those lines, sparks of light begin to awaken. See those lights growing stronger, becoming actual people of high awareness—loving, caring, serving. See yourself as a star whose rays of light and love connect with the lines of force emitted by those nearest to you. See the points everywhere become more radiant and connected. Feel yourself loving and giving, being blessed and re-energized. You are a world server in the network of loving beings.

Take a breath, and as you prepare to gently return to an awareness of the room about you, express gratitude for the experience of life, the inner spark, and the high consciousness at work within you, guiding you as you grow.

Again, take a breath. You are centered and confident. You know you have a purpose; you are wise and caring, blended spirit and matter. You use your innate knowledge well. Day by day you trust your experiences in life to guide you to fulfill your reasons for being. You embrace daily life comfortably, from a position of balance and harmony.

Again, a breath. As you are ready, return to your outer surroundings. You are filled with love and wisdom with which to live and serve as a child of light at work in the world of matter, a healing presence affirming planetary purpose. Deep breath. Eyes open. Closing gesture.

EXERCISE: OUR FATHER

Purpose: To deepen our understanding of the Lord's Prayer

Our Father, who art in heaven   *O Creator, who is*
                                  throughout the Universe
Om. Breath of life. Absolute, the One, Father and Mother
of all realms of sound and light. We remember our origins,
not with imperfections, but in the blessings given us by life.

Hallowed be thy name   *Let your name be set apart*
Hallowed is "holy," an inner shrine. In this presence we are
at peace. The feeling heart becomes the inner temple, and
in this holy place of inner peace we are in the presence of
the sacred name.

Thy kingdom come, thy will be done   *Come your kingdom*
Let your ideals and counsel govern us; let your will come
to pass. If the inner temple purifies the heart, this thought
purifies the mind. May the highest and finest rule our lives.

On Earth, as it is in heaven   *Let your delight be in Earth,*
                                  as it is throughout the Universe
Having released all thought and feeling, we align with the
Creator, Source of all. It is our desire, our will to be aligned.
Emptied, we allow the sound, energy, and love to vibrate
through us and bring us into harmony again, just as the
Universe is harmonized.

Give us this day our daily bread   *Give us bread for*
                                  our necessities today
We seek understanding, the faith that our needs will be met
from day to day. We remember the One, and we remember
the many, all creation. We ask for justice and compassion
for ourselves and for our world. We ask God to care for us,
even more than we care for one another.

And forgive us our debts   *And forgive us our offenses*
as we forgive our debtors   *as we have forgiven our offenders*
May we experience the same freedom from error and
wrong impression that we allow others to experience.
Loose us from our limitations as we release others from the
ties by which we limit them. We acknowledge our gift to be

compassionate and to set free. We acknowledge that we bind others, even curse and damage others. We recognize our power to release and heal one another. We ask that God deal with us kindly.

And lead us not into temptation　　　　　　*Do not let us enter into materialism*

Let us not be seduced by superficial appearances. Do not let us forget life is more than the surface reveals. (In Aramaic, the language of Jesus, there is no insinuation of anyone outside leading us to temptation; it is saying, do not let appearances cause us to forget the Self.) Let not pain and struggle overcome us.

But deliver us from evil　　　　　　　　　*Set us free from error*

We would not forget our source, our origins in the blessings of the Father-Mother. We would not be out of synchronization, out of fullness, or out of the light of God's Holy Plan for humankind. We share in the Oneness. Although in sympathy with the small and separate, we know that is not all. We return to the truth.

For thine is the kingdom,　　　　　　　*Because yours is the*
and the power　　　　　　　　　*kingdom, and the power,*
　　　　　　　　　　　and the song from age to age

We return to the beginning thoughts: "For to you, O great thou who art," belong the purpose, the principles, and the powers—the life-force—to accomplish the work and song of life. (We find a paradox: the God-Within and the God-Without unite, renewing the song, moment to moment, age to age.)

And the glory forever.　　　　　　　*Sealed in faithfulness*
Amen.　　　　　　　　　　　*and truth. Amen.*

More than saying, "It is so," the covenant is the moment of great affirmation. We say, *"I affirm this with my whole being."* Healing—making life whole, purposeful—is affirmed. It is as it has been, always, here and now. Again, we know it is so.　　Amen.

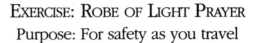

EXERCISE: ROBE OF LIGHT PRAYER
Purpose: For safety as you travel

Bless me, O Lord, this day as I clothe myself in a robe of light, composed of the love, the light, and the power of God, not only for my own protection as I travel, but so that all who come in contact may be drawn to God and assisted. Use me, Father-Mother God, to the utmost capacity for restoring the Plan on Earth. Amen.
We are all pilgrims on a journey. We pray for our planet to ascend to new and higher vibrations, our country moving toward increasingly right-guided leadership, and for ourselves as we move to greater wisdom.
May I be open to the guidance of spirit and the benefits that come to a listening member of humanity.
Sound the *Om* in closing.

EXERCISE: GROWING WITH A GROUP
Purpose: To form a group oversoul

Let us turn our attention inward, taking a breath and relaxing our attention from outer activities. Give the body the command to let go, yet keep the mind alert and ready. Let us begin.

Slowly move your attention away from your role in the world, from your body, emotions, and thoughts. Center your attention on the soulstar. Imagine a brilliant ball of light about ten inches over your head. Recognize yourself as a center of awareness, love, and choice.

Take time to experience extending your light to others, to life, extending to the other points of light about you. Radiate—push your light outward. Feel it moving, inspiring. Now see the lights touching each other, forming one great light.

In your mind, repeat after me:
Linked with my group brothers, linked in the heart of Christ,
Infused with Christ's purpose, love, and wisdom,
It is my desire and will to eliminate the blockages to
*   spiritual awakening within me.*

Visualize a vortex of spiritual energy coming from far above your head, sweeping down through the lower vehicles, going deep into the Earth, carrying away the debris, or ash, resulting from the purification by fire. In your mind, see the group at work with a series of vortices moving through them, continuing to cleanse and clear. Imagine this cleansing as a number of showers being taken. Sense the feeling of *clean.*

Imagine yourself now illumined with light—clean, shiny, fresh, new. Image the quality you have worked upon the hardest in this latest period of time, and see it resound within you. Consciously image it within you and you within it. See it. Feel it. Know it.

As you know yourself now, embody this quality. Own it. Accept it with a new awareness of yourself incorporating this quality. You now transmit this energy or quality to the lights around you. Press it outward. You will stimulate this quality in others as you grow in your ability to express this. Breathe in. Receive the qualities others have cultivated in themselves.

The planet is vibrant with qualities of new consciousness. As each of us has magnified the qualities we needed, we have advanced the cause of all. We strengthen the will-to-good for all.

Now bring the awareness held in the ball of light over your head down into your personality identity. Own the light as the energizer of your personality, the battery of your activity, your place of inspiration or source of power. Personality is now aware of the light. See the other lights and the greater light as they merge—coworking, supporting, encouraging one another. Daily we attune to the energy pool and ask what is mine to do? How can I serve? What part do I play in the Plan for humanity?

Breathe, relax, and gradually return. Repeat after me:
May the power of the one life
  pour through the group of all true servers.
May the love of the one soul
  characterize the lives of all who seek to aid the Great Ones.
May I fulfill my part in the one work
  through self-forgetfulness, harmlessness, and right speech.

Let us now send the Om together, sharing with the world about us the power of our unified souls. Om.

Your closing gesture, please.

EXERCISE: THE FOURTH WISE ONE
Purpose: Devotion to the long journey to illumination

This meditation is prepared for your personal use, one you may use to gain experience in guiding others.

Relax, and allow the body to be peaceful. You are upon a winding path in a twilight state. In the distance you see a lighted place, too far away to distinguish details.

This might be a lighted castle or a city of light, a holy place. You know it is your destination. The light that shines from it seems starlike.

Continue toward that point of light. Along the way, you meet other travelers. Sometimes you walk together for a little while, sometimes you continue with another for a longer distance. Sometimes you walk alone.

Continue now, uphill and down. Stop and think. Rest. Find interesting experiences in which to participate. Pick up items you carry. Feel yourself sometimes a child, sometimes older.

Know that your journey carries you toward illumination, awakening to your thoughtful inner nature—sometimes as a sensitive, feeling person; sometimes strong, determined, bold—always propelled toward that distant point of light.

Rest now. The Light is the long-term goal; there is no doubt. Now think about your immediate goal. To find the Christ—to honor, to rejoice, to kneel with other initiates who have also come to participate in the Christ-presence.

Your heart rejoices as you place yourself in adoration of the Christ. You are the fourth Wise One, so grateful to have found your way.

Enter the silence—rejoicing, contemplative, in awe, and rededicated to your journey. Bless the physical body that has served you and the ego that now surrenders to the Christ.

Will you follow as a devotee of the Father-Mother? Are you ready to walk in a path of mystery and challenge, to grow on this particular path? Will the Christ shed light upon your way?

Now expand the light within your heart. Place your light in the greater light of the great archangel, Lord Christ, who guides planetary life. Our hearts are full of joy and gratitude, dedicated and pure.

Feel love, love for those who have gone before, marking a path; love for those who travel with us and share our experiences; love for those known and unknown, also upon their journeys; love for all the wayshowers who have lived before us. We rejoice in Great Love.

Having filled ourselves, we rest in this healing energy. Love restores, heals, and makes whole. Accept your role as one who has found the way. Rejoice, and give thanks for the opportunities you experience.

Become mindful of other lights awakening about you, co-workers taking their places of service. See their light and love linking with your own. Emanate a deep appreciation of all: the wise now serving and those awakening to link with them. See love flowing from the past, in the present, and reaching into the future, sustaining the Great Plan for our planet and all humanity. Be open to the love that underlies the happenings of our times. Receive the Lots Of Vital Energy needed to live a holy life of service.

As you have filled yourself with such sweet love, prepare to return to awareness of the outer world, ready to share love, positive energy, hope, and healing with others and with our planet.

Think, "Love flows through me. I am loved, and I love. I am healed, and I heal." Feel your heart radiant with love, overflowing, merging into the environment. Breathe. Be gentle as you turn your attention back to this room.

For our closing let us say The Mantram of Help.[7] As you are ready:

I am a source of Endless Love
*   centered in the Light of Love Divine.*
I seek this source in You,
*   that in humanity we may together build*
A point of Love Divine
*   and send it forth, that all who recognize its Light*
*   may build anew.   Amen.*

For additional practice, review the guided exercises in *Meditation Plus* tapes: The Lotus Meditation; Awakening the Channel; Opening the Heart Center; Finding the Inner Chamber; God, I Am

Love; Transferring the Consciousness; Experience Self-Healing; Healing Help for Others; Seven Steps for Effective Prayer; and Ladder of Lights. All would be helpful to know.

Experience New Dimensions includes these meditations: The Astral Dimension; Chalice of Knowable Things; Balancing Our Own Nature; Opening as a Healing Channel; Sharpening Perception; The Power of Guided Imagery; Back in Time; Friends in Spirit; Relationship to All Kingdoms; Coworking with Devas; I Am the Soul; and Maintaining the Light.

Two Powerful Purification Techniques

An important concept in spiritual understanding is that, just as we have a residue of waste that remains in the physical body from any food we digest, so a psychic residue from every experience lingers in our subtle bodies.

References to purification relate to the cleansing work we must undergo to clear these residues. We must overcome experiences; we must heal the wounds from which we have learned. We may need to remember, every experience leaves a vestige. This is to say, our good experiences leave residue as well as our trials. We must achieve clarity in our emotional and mental natures; our window of consciousness must be without distortion.

Therefore, in addition to the meditation course work, you may choose to do the Rainbow Bridge technique at some point. Presented in the book by that name,[8] it is a beneficial program that will mesh with the work of these lessons.

Coming to the Sunrise is a more complicated work. This set of tapes engages the senses in a powerful series of guided exercises which reveal issues to be called to the practitioner's attention. Direction, such as a time commitment, are to be followed carefully or these tapes should not be used.

If you have concerns about specific works to which you have been introduced, consider corresponding with the meditation tutors. If you have accomplished six months of dedicated effort or up to two years of passive meditation work previously, please proceed to the next lesson. If not, communicate with the tutors, who will probably ask you to do more passive work and report on your experiences.

The Impact of Meditation: Metamorphosis

First you seek the light,
next you are in the light,
then you are the light.

—Sai Baba

A s experiences of specific work meditation impact us, we become aware of our great opportunity to make a difference in our own unfolding lives and in others' lives by drawing upon subtler energies. We are gathering tools to assist others as we advance in meditation awareness.

In this lesson we begin to grasp the full panorama of meditation. Often, because we sit quietly and appear inactive, a true comprehension of its potency remains unrealized. A commitment to meditate is to embrace the long journey of evolution as a conscious participant, knowing we are eager and ready to be all that we might be. Saints and sages, Masters and teachers have cut a path for us to follow.

The qualities of self-within blend with personality to produce the new being, and this image of becoming new, or born again, brings us to the concepts of *transformation, transmutation, and transfiguration,* further discussed in volume 2. This is the process of spiritual *alchemy occurring within the denser nature. This new body, the light body, or "glory body" is the radiant form Jesus the Christ revealed on the mountain during the transfiguration.

Spiritual teachings repeatedly refer to these processes. While closely related, the terms are not synonymous; each pertains to a different stage of powerful growth.

The first work is the **transformation** of personality so that it aligns with a pattern appropriate to spiritual life. Think of this as sensitizing the disciple so the incoming spiritual forces may have impact. This is the level which modern churches try to influence. The esoteric Christian tradition, however, concerns itself with the inner work of birthing the Christ-Within, rather than the traditional approaches espousing dogma and particular denominational positions. Esoteric means "inner" or "out-of-sight." Esoteric Christians believe that Christianity as offered to humanity by Master Jesus is a transformational process to enlightenment; the teachings and practices should lead us to the transpersonal level of consciousness. This is the Divine-Within which brings us to: *Let this mind be in you, which was also in Christ Jesus* (Philippians 2.5), so that ultimately we may each be able to say, *I and my Father are one* (John 10.30).

While most Christians focus upon the outer or exoteric tradition, the time will come in their growth and individuation when they will demand more of their religious practice than words and songs. They will want to penetrate the holy space where transformation occurs. Chanting the rosary produces a vibration that allows the inner processes to cleanse and clear and energizes change. This is just part of a larger lifestyle for the serious spiritual student, but it is an empowering part. Here we leave religious tradition and begin to deal with spiritual practices. The religious gives us keys and guides the outer life by dogma. The essence of self will ultimately seek food to satisfy its own hunger.

Meditation is a powerful tool to increase sensitivity to higher vibrations. Energizing personality with high and holy words of power increases our response to higher influences. The light evoked stimulates the light of the cells, or dense body; the light of spirit and the matter of physical life move toward balance. The effects are those of healing, increased sensitivity, development of astral senses, and flashes of intuition. A certain radiance manifests.

This invocation of spiritual energy also clears and cleanses the astral and mental vehicles. As the astral reflects the feelings and the mind focuses upward, their refined frequencies capture and reflect the higher. Devotion fills the astral vehicle with love and energies of the soul, and negative emotions are neutralized or released; love fills the life as higher aspirations begin to guide. As light penetrates the mental vehicles, illusions that obscure clear-seeing and the wisdom of the higher Plan dissolve. The mind more faithfully reflects the High Self level of awareness, facilitating the cleansing work; heart, mind, and body begin to harmonize. The aspirant keeps self charged with light, love, and spiritual power for the purpose of transforming the physical life.

Transmutation is the process of reworking the physical, emotional, and mental levels of personality through changes in the very substance of the vehicles. As cleansing each level takes place, an actual transmutation from matter to light occurs. The body, now much more reflective of heart and mind, gradually becomes a delicate receiver set for high frequencies. The refined emotional nature becomes a reflective source of energy that responds enthusiastically to flashes of light from the higher.

As the holy names and words of spiritual power are spoken in a contemplative, devotional, quiet, and sincere manner, both matter and consciousness vibrate to a higher frequency. The instrument adjusts or adapts to handle the frequencies the individual is evoking. In other words, the etheric counterpart of the physical vehicle becomes clearer and has more impact upon the physical receiver set. The aura around the aspirant increases in its glow or vibrancy.

H.P. Blavatsky[1] said, "*Manas is spiritual self-consciousness." This higher consciousness cannot express itself in the lower world without a reflective device. It is our human mind, or lower manas, which serves as that device. It is therefore the task of the lower manas, thinking personality, to paralyze and dissipate the properties of the physical, or material, form which obstruct the light. It is the *kama-manas, the lower ego, that would be deluded into the false belief of independent existence.

As the illusion of human intelligence diminishes, the mind that is in Christ Jesus evolves. This is the mind that thinketh in the heart, also spoken of as the heart behind the heart. Feeling (heart) and knowing (mind) blend, transmuting the receiving vehicles and imbuing them with harmonious abilities dedicated to service. The abilities of the spiritual disciple are disclosed. "Greater works than these shall ye do"[2] becomes a true potential, rather than wishful thinking. This mind, attuned to Divine Mind, is a result of the transmuting process.

Extended consciousness builds the thread connecting the higher manas with the kama-manas, producing a spirit-filled consciousness living within matter. The power of the human ego may then cleanse personality of confusion, distortion, and error (sin) if it so chooses. It becomes a real effort for the sincere disciple to do this cleansing for the self; it is a great work for awakened ones on behalf of the many in a time when there is so much to do, and so few to do it.

As invocation continues, the **transfiguration** from human to divine follows. The new Adam, or God-man, is born.

—Carol Parrish-Harra, *The Aquarian Rosary*[3]

Master Jesus revealed himself in his glory form in the transfiguration experience on the mountaintop. This is considered the third initiation step in Esoteric Christianity. We, too, will be transfigured ultimately, a being both human and divine. In our study we use "soul-infused personality" to indicate this level of achievement at which soul can radiate its bright light through the sheaths of personality. This radiance reveals the light, love, and power of the soul at work; personality has surrendered to the soul, and the human nature has adapted to the soul qualities.

Now we see how humanity struggles with these three steps in our spiritual evolution. First, **transformation:** we transform our lives to live as ethical human beings. We invoke will, choose our religion or our path and reform our lives to accommodate its strictures. We try to reflect the highest consciousness we understand, obediently living in that awareness day to day. At this level of understanding, we use concepts of right and wrong, good and bad, as well as the dictates of denominations, to help determine personal boundaries.

Next, **transmutation** occurs. We change; the ethers of the astral (emotional) nature adjust as interaction happens day by day with the potentized energies of higher mind. Transmutation of the astral nature and the mental bodies takes place, and even the physical body becomes more androgynous.

Each human being has a unique frequency and chemical make-up. Upon blending the heart (astral nature) and mind (mental nature), they become new in nature because neither remains the same. New abilities emerge that were not a part of the old. The purified emotional nature expresses itself as a powerful battery to urge the divine potential of the mental nature. Aspiration and potential merge into new abilities.

The third step: **transfiguration,** the little-understood mystery of soul-infused personality, is the great goal of this stage of human evolution. How can the human manas (intelligence) attune itself to the energies of the soul and then allow soul to use personality as its vessel? This transfiguration process lies at the heart of the Christian message; it is the central theme of the discipline of Agni Yoga, which was introduced earlier and about which you will learn more in future lessons.

> *This new body, the light body,*
> *or "glory body," is the radiant form*
> *Jesus the Christ revealed*
> *on the mountain*
> *during the transfiguration.*

In transfiguration, the goal is to evolve a cohesive consciousness within our own etheric head centers, the spiritual triad (more fully explained in volume 3). This reference point attunes to the fiery mind of God, as registered in the Cloud of Knowable Things—a collection of related pieces of information, ideas, blueprints, or even poetic expression formed at the intuitive and abstract level—and is attracted to the seed thought. The focused attention is used like a stick to bat the piñata. Once pierced, the feeling, thought, or flow just tumbles earthward or, should we say, mindward. "For our God is a consuming fire" (Hebrews 12.29) reminds us of light and purification, the burning away of all that cannot become one, and we know how profoundly fire has changed human life.

> Someday, after we have mastered the winds, the waves, the tides and gravity, we will harness for God the energies of love—and then, for the second time in the history of the world, man will have discovered fire!
>
> —Father Teilhard de Chardin

I like to call disciplined creativity the foundation of transfiguration. The fires of purification have completed their work in both heart and mind, and the glory body is being formed—transfiguration. We need to recall this powerful promise by rereading scriptures that tell us why we seek the inner self:

Whoever from now on is a follower of Christ is a new creation.

2 Corinthians 5.17

What is born of flesh is flesh; and what is born of the Spirit is spirit. Do not be surprised because I have told you that you all must be born again.

John 3.6,7

Being born again, not of corruptible seed, but of incorruptible, by the word of God, which lives and abides for ever.

1 Peter 1.23

Similarly, Master Jesus is revealed in his glory body (transfigured) to three of his disciples:

And Jesus taketh Peter, James, and John his brother and bringeth them up into an high mountain apart. And was transfigured before them: and his face did shine as the sun; and his raiment was white as the light.

Matthew 17.1,2

And Christ, speaking of John bearing witness to the truth, said:

He was a burning and a shining light.

John 5.35

We hold high aspirations, knowing they will be fulfilled in time. Meditation then is creative thinking through the light of intuition to harmonize the outer with the potential held in the divine Plan. We are to travel from level to level and register the beauties, the knowledge, the richness of each level, then bring them down to the human plane to serve humanity. We are to open new pathways to the unknown to make them known for those who will travel after us.

For those who would guide humanity into the future, the purpose is not to seek joy or happiness, to be lost in supreme silence, or to merge with the whole, but rather to see the Plan and to prepare to serve as implementers. The Plan is often called the "will of the Creator."

To do this work, we must realize the unity of the Cosmos, to encompass it and to register the progressive steps to unfoldment. True meditation leads to an acute awareness of the whole and our relationship to the great drama of life.

Meditation refines and perfects our expression. We become capable of communication between newly discovered realities, energies, and beauties, as well as the Great Life as a whole. Again and again, our mind must open to higher realities and register the lofty impressions we find.

As new, subtler energies are contacted, they create temporary upheaval in the physical, emotional, and mental bodies as the age-old grime, long hidden, rises to the surface to be recognized and washed away. This is happening when we learn to say sincerely, "Forgive them, they know not what they do."

Saraydarian suggests the practice of meditation moves us from **inertia** to **action** (motion) to **harmony** (rhythm). He says we are to think of this as moving from the power of 50 (50x) to the power of 500 (500x) to the power of 5000 (5000x); with each multiplication we vibrate at a higher frequency with the Plan. While we are never standing still in our spiritual growth, 50x may seem like "still" to one vibrating to 5000x. Those vibrating rapidly to the Plan, should they fall into comparison to one moving slowly, might consider the slower-moving to be a straggler or unawakened; but, indeed, those who appear to be standing still may have all they can manage. Their challenges seem as great to them at that vibration of 50x as the challenges of the more advanced 5000x seem to those experiencing that high-level vibration.

Any discerning teacher may guide us to think of personality as living in inertia, soul as living in motion, and the God-Spark as living in rhythm. As awakened ones, we strive to vibrate to the frequency of the soul and become charged with the energy of higher consciousness. As we take on this soul energy, life is seen differently, lived differently, and valued in a new way. At later stages of growth, the Soul will be challenged to vibrate to the "electric fire" of the Spark which now is almost impossible for us to imagine. We often call this divine spark the "*monad." It is the essence of our divine nature, that which truly belongs to the Fiery World, the "I-am consciousness."

To proceed with meditation of a high reality, beyond relaxation and pure satisfaction, we must develop three essential qualities:

Humility. Surrendering to our part in the plan.

Cooperation. Learning to be part of the group, aiding the group work, and sharing in its karma.

Gratitude. Being thankful and appreciative for each opportunity to work as a representative of the higher world. Gratitude, one of the heart energies, is closely akin to healing.

Each of these qualities has its own special demands. Humility necessitates surrendering. Cooperation links us with the aspiration and purposes of others. Gratitude develops values, obligations, and responsibilities. Having acquired these qualities, we are now enabled to work for the soul's purpose, rather than the ego's desires.

True meditation is a redemptive process which reverses the current of materialism and lifts us toward spiritualization. Because meditation awakens unfinished business in the individual and in the group, will we become aware of personal imperfections and work to align ourselves to the vision that guides us, as well as to the group of which we are a part. As the purification work is fulfilled, the group and the individual discover more peace of mind, beauty, and nobility of spirit.

An advantage to being part of a group is that others help us hold the positive energy, while one by one the personal work is achieved. When we align with a high vision, we sustain it and it sustains the workers.

The familiar five-pointed star, or pentagram, is often used to represent the awakened human because it reminds us of the five significant areas of life to be mastered: physical, emotional, mental, spiritual, and social (group life).

The pure consciousness of the "I Am," the inner divinity, resides well veiled by personality's particular strengths and weaknesses. In the hope of realizing enlightenment, each of us must face barriers to the liberated state. As the soul, we create our journey, constructing many ego defenses, habits of operation, and distortions.

As we set our sights upon the goal of illumination, we settle down to the work with great intensity. Each bold adventurer has virtues to develop and undesirable traits to clear. Obstacles to the path must be met by those who seek what is known as the path of redemption, the initiatory path. To make specific progress, psycho-spiritual work is undertaken with dedication.

Dysfunction at a higher level (mind, perhaps) brings consequences to the lower level (body, perhaps) by producing experiences of pain and confusion through which lessons are precipitated.

The time arrives to dissolve the barriers to the Self. Each area of personality distortion must be discovered. Each barrier to high consciousness must be transformed into a clear lens through which new perspective may be perceived. Remember, in growth no lower levels are lost; they align under the direction of the new, higher understanding.

As we ascend the Pyramid of Meditation (see figure i.), we are dedicated to building a consciousness that responds to specific spiritual technology. We become sensitive both to information from our own extended senses and to ways of utilizing these senses. Now we face the challenges engendered by seeking to dissolve the barriers to enlightenment found in personality. Step by step, the work outlined in these lessons is designed to clear away

cobwebs of confusion and distortion of which you may or
may not be aware presently.

Perform the techniques introduced to you sincerely and
conscientiously, for they are indeed powerful. They are ages old
and have proven themselves highly effective in the changing of
consciousness. Embrace the work with persistence, knowing Spirit
will respond sensitively to your needs. Remember, the energy of
meditation has been proven scientifically to restore psychological
well-being, to heal physical bodies, and to reduce crime.

The Masters teach:

- watch the ugliness of the world, but see its beauty;
- realize you are surrounded by darkness, but stay in
  communion with the inner light;
- know that waves of unrest knock upon the outer shores of
  physical life, but that they are anchored to inner reality.

Thus meditation brings about a continuous expansion of
consciousness. This decisive technique raises the vibration of
human life so that it may co-exist in harmony with the will of the
Creator.

The impact of meditation is to strengthen the aura and restore
balance if practiced correctly. Its effects influence the profession or
occupation of the practitioner; it flows into the environment,
allowing those who establish inner connection to become a
blessing to their family, home, and, in outer expression, through
creativity, career, or service.

In meditation, we ascend through levels of reality and then
absorb into our aura the residue of what we have touched. A
mixture of our personality, reactions, feelings, and thoughts sur-
rounds us and creates an atmosphere of enclosure. As we persist
in the practice of relaxation and then centering, we find the seed
of potentiality awaiting inside that field of calm, clear space reserved for
personal development. We quiet the scanning rational mind and, lo, we
discover that quiescent self at our light center, peaceful and potent.
Having once located this point (see figure 4), with practice, we will find
it more easily. Gradually we will learn how to derive personality
guidance from our higher nature through passive meditation. Those
who effectively work with passive techniques are then encouraged to
learn another new way: active meditation.

The soul unfolds itself like a lotus of countless petals.
—Kahlil Gibran, *The Prophet*

This "active" step bypasses the astral dimension to leap upward in frequency and contact the mental plane. The tool used for this contact is a seed thought that vibrates to a faster frequency in a higher field of thought. Practitioners of these techniques continue to build the mental body in order to enter the *Halls of Learning in the unseen worlds where they are assisted by an inner teacher. Using such practices, they begin to contact the intuitive realities by which humanity has long been guided, and the intensity of their meditation precipitates droplets that inspire, teach, and transmute their own natures. This precipitation is holy thought flowing from the Source (Lord Christ, the holy one). This downpouring stimulates the aspirant to pray, to talk to God-Transcendent. We think of this as crying out the deepest prayer of the fervent heart. The doors to life behind the veil may now be opened.

As we contact the energies of the soul (the intuitive reality), these influences penetrate the mind. The mental body develops gradually, level by level, and those prepared become increasingly aware of the Plan projected toward humanity. The Plan itself is gradually stepped into form by those who perceive the part they can indeed perform.

According to the level of energy we contact, we adjust to vibrate accordingly. We are lifted to a new frequency as we touch the energy of the soul, and it reorganizes our subtle bodies. Long-awaited spiritual potentials stir and make themselves known. We become both more sensitive and increasingly stimulated by these new currents.

People Change When They Meditate

The process of meditation is one of purification, healing, and alignment. Purification and healing take place as we recover from the scars of past experience, old programming, and maya. When we find that inner calm, our work becomes releasing, restructuring, and repairing our nature. In time, the new is realized.

A simple but noble way to think about levels of consciousness comes to us from the *Huna tradition. We call upon it to help us understand levels of self as we begin. In later lessons, as we begin to see the wonders of the mind's potential unfolding, refinement occurs.

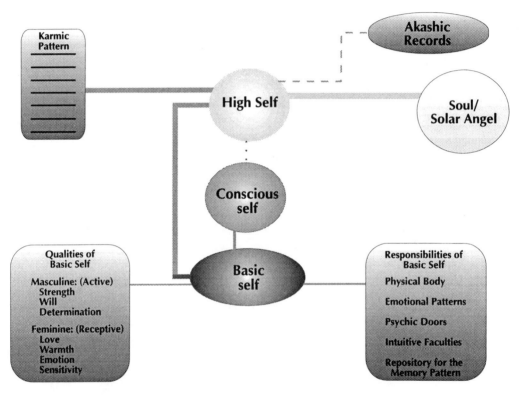

Figure 14. Personality's Perspective.

Much of our awareness has slipped beneath our consciousness and is held in the basic self. As the human evolved, the instinctual nature, with its emphasis on survival, its acute animal senses, and its fight-or-flight syndrome, shifted to lower priority; however, as we learn in times of emergency or sudden developmental spurts, it resurfaces.

This basic nature possesses capabilities we rarely focus upon until we begin to *know thyself* in some new way. The basic self brings us messages from our higher nature through codes that range from dreams to stomachaches. The innate intelligence is ingenious at providing dramas and symbols to convey its information, although only a limited amount may ever be understood consciously.

Practices   **Results**

As prayer and
meditation begin. . . . . .new insight and awareness begin.
We see the Plan and know.
We find our inner guidance.
We penetrate the Cloud
of Knowable Things.

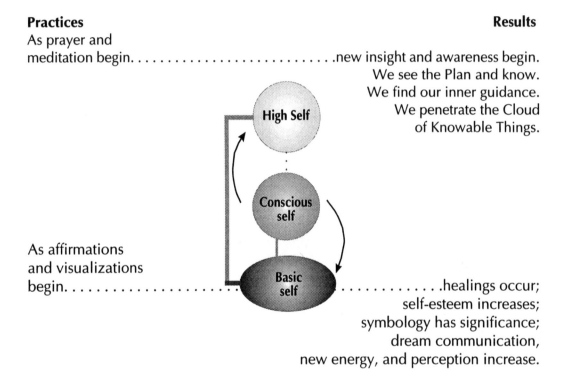

As affirmations
and visualizations
begin. . . . . .healings occur;
self-esteem increases;
symbology has significance;
dream communication,
new energy, and perception increase.

Figure 15. The Impact of Spiritual Practices Well Done.

We do, however, learn to communicate from conscious self to basic self and from conscious self to High Self (higher consciousness) as we raise our consciousness. Early steps usually include affirmations and visualizations to communicate with the basic self and prayer and meditation as techniques for invoking the assistance of High Self.

Communication between levels of self is the net result of expansion of consciousness. We learn to access information by shifting levels from chakra to chakra or adjusting brain-wave frequencies. Both scientific means and spiritual means are available to assist our exploration. Biofeedback, with its research into brain-wave cycles and substantiated explanations, may be the best source of data for those seeking a scientific route. Spiritual practitioners usually develop their inner perception through spiritual disciplines and a personal practice, blending their religious and cultural heritage. However, as perception sharpens, we sense we are being led. As the adage suggests, *When the student is ready, the teacher appears.*

So, as we proceed with personal development, we recall the biblical example of the Last Supper. We place ourselves at the lower end of the table; the host, the Christ, invites us to move higher, closer to him as we are ready. When we begin anew, we enter at the most modest levels and allow the spirit within to manifest itself by moving us rapidly forward. It is good for both ego and spirit.

As we lead spiritual lives, even challenges are seen as experiences drawn to us for the purpose of growth. We do not bemoan our karma. This river of life lifts and moves us unconsciously toward the Source. Awakened, we struggle to raise our consciousness to reflect a new and wiser perspective.

> God is the spring and the source of all goodness and flows over into all creatures—God is the main river and creatures are the tributaries of goodness.
> —Thomas Aquinas, *Contra Gentes*

We need to realize that not all meditation is productive, particularly guided imagery practiced without higher purpose, and indeed these do cause difficulties for a limited number of practitioners. For this reason, meditation was formerly taught only in the mystery schools under the watchful eyes of those who had experience and could demonstrate wisdom and readiness to guide others—such as our tutors.

During recapitulation, we often awaken "sleeping" karma. For example, once a student I knew well persisted in asking what previous relationship she had experienced with her newborn son whom she loved so dearly. She became obsessed with knowing. One day she succeeded in seeing him in her mind as an abusive, tyrannical father whom she hated. When the experience ended, she felt quite different about her child. Her affection dried up and, in fact, she let her parents raise him. The opportunity to love and heal was lost. Students are cautioned to go slowly: "Don't push the river." Allow wisdom to gain momentum before stirring too deeply. Also, seek guidance from wise ones when issues do surface.

Meditation creates a rush of energy through which lives move and change rapidly, in keeping with how the Great Life experiences it. Rather than seeing challenges as personal, we find ourselves facing the challenges of the world, knowing each small part of consciousness reflects the Great Life ever more clearly as the personal "stuff" is cleared.

Meditation delivers the grace the world needs, that homes need, that humanity needs to facilitate the experience of evolving. Meditation is the pipeline, the lifeline, the sustaining technique of being in touch with the Plan for humanity one by one and collectively. As personal karma is completed, each disciple seeks to dissolve some share of the group karma, hoping to hasten the day humanity will transcend its current level of understanding.

Instructions here are simplified; they will gradually become more elaborate, more complex and complete as your experience increases and deepens.

Seed-Thought Meditation Procedure

1. We begin with preparation techniques. If you have been doing quiet-time work already, you may now find it easy to enter a deeply relaxed state almost immediately, i.e., alpha. As you begin, place yourself in posture and see the soulstar over your head radiating its light toward you, shining upon you. Bathed in the light, filled with the light, you are ready to begin this new work.

The following procedure prepares you for seed-thought work. Direct your attention to the seed thought, the word provided for each lesson. Our first word will be "expansion."

← E—X—P—A—N—S—I—O—N →

2. Look intently at the word for a few seconds, then close your eyes. Mentally say something like, "I seek the meaning behind this word (phrase, sentence, or symbol)."

A word is dehydrated thought. When we look up any word in the dictionary, we find additional words to define it. As we meditate upon a word or symbol, the mind expands the meaning, bringing more awareness to the seed thought. Think of Spirit reconstituting this dehydrated thought to give you greater awareness of its fuller meaning.

3. Place the symbol—the word—in the center of your mind. See it. Mentally repeat it several times, forcefully at first. Then think the word less forcefully, and finally say it quietly.

Allow the word to become a mantra. See it, hear it, allow it to make an impact. Note your feelings in response to the word. Sense it as a vibration or impulse. Is it alive and vibrant or soft and restful? The subtle vibration you sense is called the "quality." What quality does the word emit?

Holding the word in your mind, focus your attention first upon one letter, then another. Perhaps "expansion" moves in your mind's eye, i.e., surges or begins to dance. Perhaps it now feels dynamic, adventurous, or even pulsating. Then, holding "expansion" in your mind's eye, observe it growing and growing until you cannot contain the size of it. You may be ready now to interact mentally with the seed thought.

4. As you hold the word in your mind, ask a series of questions about it. Pause after each one to see what impressions appear in your conscious awareness. Continue with these thoughts as long as they emerge. You may repeat the question, trying to penetrate more deeply. If a blank period occurs, ask the next question and repeat the process.

Key questions:
   a. How do I experience this word, or how does it express in the world?
   b. What is its nature, its essence?
   c. What is its immediate and ultimate source?
   d. Why does this essence exist?
Allow each flow of thought or feeling to carry you as far as it will.

You need not go through each question each session; one question may occupy the entire time. In fact, you need not feel compelled to use the questions at all. As the flow of inner meanings begins, just attempt to capture the essence directly. This is a dynamic process, not intended to be cut-and-dried or repetitive. Every word has an energy, a feeling, a vibration of its own. Note that, and you will have begun. Follow the process as you can, registering your thoughts and feelings. Capture as much as possible from the experience.

5. As you ask questions about the word, make a distinct but relaxed effort to push into the realm of true knowing, tapping the fundamental knowledge of which the word is only an outward symbol. Imagine you are moving to examine the word from every angle. Feel yourself open to accept the knowledge which might come as words, pictures, images, sounds, patterns, melodies, feelings of movement, abstract symbols, impressions, even tastes or smells.

The sense of push is an acknowledgement of your will to focus, an important component of active meditation. You are focused, alert, pressing into the thought, a sense of lifting upward. In turn, the word acts upon your consciousness.

6. As you feel a desire to do so, record whatever you receive in any form that seems appropriate. Jot down your thoughts and feelings, your impressions. These are so fleeting, they quickly evaporate, and usually we do not realize how much we have received if they are not recorded. As happens when we write down our dreams, more begins to impinge upon the mind as we write, so that we often recall even subtler thoughts. The more we capture impressions, the more we seem to draw additional thoughts. They may come as something we see, a drawing or an abstraction that represents a complexity difficult to put into words. As we record and new insights emerge, we "go with the flow." This written record

may be done during the process or at the end of the session, so keep pen and paper at hand. As you become experienced at capturing your perceptions, your arm will seem to become a mere extension of your mind. Your thoughts will stream rapidly onto the note pad without disrupting your focused mind. In fact, you will become aware how easily this happens. Do not think up something; simply record the delicate touches of thought that come to mind. Do not be concerned with sentences and form. Just capture those subtle touches. As you do more of this, it becomes increasingly easy to stimulate the process.

One student shared these impressions:

It is a difficult task bringing wordless, expansive concepts into limited, contracted words. No sooner is it done than a box is drawn around the words. The practical mystic must help erase the box, choosing words of expansion to aid the receiving, opening aspirants. Not only is this information given to aspirants, but to the rest of the world as well. Sometimes when the words are misinterpreted, there arises great anxiety among individuals or groups. The mystic makes corrections whenever possible, but the thoughtforms remain, waiting to be neutralized by the meditation service of others.

—Rev. Jan Skogstrom[4]

7. At the conclusion of the meditation, allow a few moments to return to your usual outer-world consciousness and regain a sense of balance. Express gratitude for what you have received. Then open your eyes, and become aware of the sights and sounds around you, feeling alert and refreshed before rising and going about your daily life.

Such a session is best limited to fifteen to thirty minutes. For our structured course work, use each seed thought about fifteen times (or days) before proceeding to the next. This is merely a recommended number of times. You may "run dry" after seven or ten sessions; other times you may wish to continue until you feel you are no longer getting further depth.

An Abbreviated Seed-Thought Meditation

1. Preparatory chanting, singing, or music. Begin to relax.

2. Read a brief piece of devotional material.

3. Continue to relax. Close your eyes, and turn your attention within.

4. Become aware of a light (your soulstar) over your head.

5. Draw the soulstar energy to your heart. Magnify your feelings of love-caring. Allow the love to flow. Feel it move through your emotional nature—clearing, cleansing, nurturing. Let go of past and future. Be here now, in the healing flow of the moment. See the body filled with light, and love it for the service it renders.

6. Breathe, and move your attention to the mind.

7. Lift your magnetized focus into the Cloud of Knowable Things.

8. Begin to focus upon your seed thought: "_____"

9. Capture the thoughts you have contacted, then recite the Great Invocation (see Appendix). Speak it, working "as if" you are a soul-infused personality, both as doing service and as thankfulness for that which you have received.

10. Conclude this work by speaking the sacred tone, *Om,* aloud three times.

To summarize, spiritual traditions accept those who present themselves for training as seekers because they are ready to be made new. They are given simple exercises that begin the revitalizing of the three brains that guide humanity, knowing that in due time any necessary repairs will be made; when ready, the three will synchronize, and the aspirant will embrace high consciousness.

Thus techniques are undertaken to strengthen the reptilian brain. As we continue our recapitulation, we soon add practices to rebuild the mammalian connection. Most of us have no difficulty with left hemisphere requirements of the cerebral neocortex, but what about the right? Our relationship to the greater must become real. We must awaken new senses and find new comprehension.

We practice passive meditation techniques to facilitate interaction between the two that each might share its own particular resources.

As you practice seed-thought meditation, you might want to recall that its greatest purpose is to increase your conscious contact with inner reality. Think of it as lifting your mind to press against higher mind; at the same time, be receptive to subtle, sometimes delicate thoughts that come.

Let us rethink the work to be done as we align ourselves to the soul. This assignment begins our seed-thought work and advances us to level 3 which will give us an overview of what occurs out of sight as progress in meditation builds the mental body. A great and sacred work is embraced as we begin active meditation.

Assignment

Seed Thought: Expansion

Expanses divine my soul craves.
Confine me not in cages,
of substance or of spirit.
—Abraham Isaac Kook

For what may be your initial experience with the active approach to meditation, follow the procedure on page 145. Your first seed thought, the focus of your effort, is *Expansion*. While a seed thought can be one word, a phrase, or a sentence (even a lengthy sentence in certain instances), now we will use only one word. Since you will be working with this word approximately fifteen times, maintain a record of your thoughts, insights, and experiences in a designated notebook. Be sure to date each session. In time, your journal will form the basis of your report to your tutor.

You have reached Level 3

The Piscean Age made Divinity human;
the Aquarian Age will make humanity divine.
—William Gray, kabalist

As we ascend the pyramid, we continue to monitor our personality and do the work required for change to lead us forward. We comprehend the evolution—forced growth—stimulated by meditation, for we know the needs of each brain, as well as its contribution to the collective growth of humankind. We practice formality and repetition, movement and rhythms; we discover freshness and are filled with wonder for each new day. Quietly centered and observing, we gain information and insights, a witness to life itself unfolding wondrously.

We are the people of the future living today, attuned and ready for the intuitive flash. The stream of inner knowing guides us; we are drawing upon the special awareness we have reaped through day-to-day practice. Personality approaches the temple; soul awaits. How do we come to the teacher? Respectfully. How do we advance in the teachings? With purity, as clear as possible. We approach our goal one step at a time with confidence at having come thus far.

The Tibetan advises:
Meditation is dangerous and unprofitable to the man who enters upon it without the basis of a good character and of clean living. . . . Meditation is dangerous where there is wrong motive, such as desire for personal growth and for spiritual powers, for under these conditions it produces only a strengthening of the shadows in the vale of illusion and brings to full growth the serpent of pride, lurking in the valley of selfish desire. Meditation is dangerous when the desire to serve is lacking.
—Alice A. Bailey
A Treatise on White Magic[5]

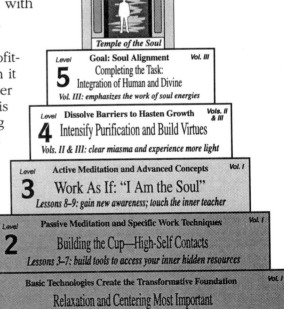

SOUL

Temple of the Soul

Level		
5	**Goal: Soul Alignment** Completing the Task: Integration of Human and Divine	Vol. III
	Vol. III: emphasizes the work of soul energies	

Level		
4	**Dissolve Barriers to Hasten Growth** Intensify Purification and Build Virtues	Vols. II & III
	Vols. II & III: clear miasma and experience more light	

Level		
3	**Active Meditation and Advanced Concepts** Work As If: "I Am the Soul"	Vol. I
	Lessons 8–9: gain new awareness; touch the inner teacher	

Level		
2	**Passive Meditation and Specific Work Techniques** Building the Cup—High-Self Contacts	Vol. I
	Lessons 3–7: build tools to access your inner hidden resources	

Level		
1	**Basic Technologies Create the Transformative Foundation** Relaxation and Centering Most Important	Vol. I
	Lessons 1–2: know humanity's process and create a solid foundation for your inner life	

Meditation, the Great Service

Even Master Jesus, the Christ, withdrew and entered into solitude and silence to refill his cup, that he could persevere in his service. We must remember, humanity exists in a dense atmosphere of pollution and peril. Our work is to hold tight to the umbilical cord that connects us to the Holy. That lifeline is meditation.

Through humanity's alignment to meditation at this time, certain immediate goals are being revealed to move us toward the emerging golden age. Meditation charges initiates with the spiritual dedication to complete the work they undertake. Some of these goals are:

- to reveal the subjective synthesis in humanity
- to establish a great station of light to illumine the realm of human thought
- to restore the mysteries of initiation
- to facilitate incoming new energies for healing, cleansing, harmonizing, and for the restoration of values and virtues
- to bring to an end the age-long spirit of separativeness
- to further systems of intercommunication and interrelationship through telepathy and the science of impression
- to bring about a closer, more direct, and more conscious cooperation between the Masters of the race and the servers of the race.
- to train servers to be responsive to the Plan.

These are but a few of the works meditation leads us to undertake. All is dependent upon sincerity of heart and readiness of mind that cause us to fall on our knees and say, *All is ready, Master, come.*

Know What
the Soul Knows

There is nothing more potent than thought.
Deed follows word and word follows thought.
The world is the result of a mighty thought,
and where the thought is mighty and pure,
the result is always mighty and pure.

—Mahatma Gandhi

Active meditation is a development technique to stretch our mental capability toward new possibilities. We strive to lift our minds to touch Divine Mind. Pressing against higher mind, we allow that connection to register upon our mental mechanism.

Here we knock at the door of higher consciousness, lift the mind with its seed thought, and ask to be taught by Divine Mind. Thus, the soul level of self is sought, for an awareness of the great Plan exists in the soul. The soul seeks to share its wisdom through contact. *Knock and it shall be opened* reminds us we must *ask* to receive. Our spiritual efforts create ways to ask.

Spirituality is the expression of the essence of oneself. As attention is focused upon our innermost dimension, the essence—called self, soul, or spirit by most esoteric traditions—opens and shares its transcendental nature. Spiritual practices are designed to evoke and explore this essence and give it greater freedom of expression. This "sacred within" can then interface its dimensions with personality.

Line of Being and Line of Knowing

Consciousness advances along two major parallel lines of development: the line of knowledge and the line of being. In steady progress these two tracks develop simultaneously, each advancing and enriching the other. We learn something, we integrate it into our experience, and the experience confirms the truth of what we have learned. Comprehension and integration earn advancement on the line of knowledge, not mere accumulation of data.

Our level of beingness advances when we honor our own essence. This growth depends upon our living what we "know," overtly or subjectively. The authenticity of our life depends upon the awareness we carry, which in turn determines our quality of life. We often sense integrity in the simplest lives because the personality of such lives is not splintered by conflicting roles or cultural struggles. Perhaps such people haven't had to absorb any more information than they are able to integrate; or perhaps their hearts and minds have not been at conflict. The line of being affirms wholeness with whatever experience arises.

A complication in this modern era of opportunity is that so much can be known, so much information can be accessed without becoming knowledge. If we grasp a piece of information, examine and experience it to determine what it has to offer, we can then know it because this confirmed reality is more easily integrated into our real being. However, when too much information comes to us without sufficient time to make it our own, our quality of being fails to keep pace. Living in a time when we are inundated with data, we must recognize that saturating our intellect is much like over-eating. The conscious mind becomes greedy for all it can capture without digesting and integrating what it has already acquired.

What is called the line of beingness advances more naturally in slower-moving periods. We gather information, experiment with it, and witness to our understanding. If we are apprenticed to a mentor, we must prove ourselves before the mentor permits us access to more information.

All of this occurs unconsciously. With the current bombardment of information, unless we focus on one line of development, we may be inundated with data that distracts our purpose and impedes our life direction. Tests will still come to validate the level of knowledge we have truly acquired; similarly, we will undergo trials to define our quality of being.

In the midst of daily life, being our honorable selves affirms our spirituality. We may know more or less than another, but spirituality has to do with the ethics of applying our knowledge. Beingness has to do with qualities of self we bring to life situations and the integration of levels of self in practical, honorable, and serving ways.

The line of knowledge is ultimately determined by our ability to *be*. This is easily forgotten or discredited by a culture that values knowledge (really information) above being. A ready example in our modern era is the amount of investment—intelligence, time, attention, money—that went into the development of nuclear power before a solution was determined for the disposal of the nuclear waste we were creating. Accumulation of knowledge has the potential to obscure our being. Too much information can confuse us or cause us to doubt important aspects of our being. The line of being advances as we apply our knowledge to daily living correctly.

> *The authenticity of our life*
> *depends upon the awareness we carry,*
> *which in turn determines our quality of life.*

Spiritual teachings and meditation experiences help us forgive, release, and better understand ourselves and others. They affirm us and help us align to and work through the inevitable trials of life. When we hold beliefs as dogma, not integrated by contemplation, such beliefs generally do not penetrate our being, and we are left with a line of information (rather than knowledge) and an allegiance to maya. True being does not gain the momentum to advance.

As we proceed in these lessons, you will be introduced to techniques requiring your introspection, as well as the absorption of a massive amount of information. The information and techniques for application of the process propel us toward the great

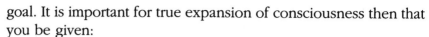

goal. It is important for true expansion of consciousness then that you be given:

1. Information that becomes knowledge;
2. Meditation techniques for the strengthening of spiritual muscle;
3. New awareness gathered from the use of seed thoughts;
4. Ways to integrate these qualities (virtues) into your being; and,
5. Usable knowledge for experiential application.

So, we see our effort to expand consciousness with active meditation consists of both penetration into the Cloud of Knowable Things, contacting concepts, and bringing them back for contemplation. We must blend the knowledge offered and the thoughts contacted into our daily lifestyle. A word of caution: do not hurry. This is a process, not a contest. Academic work is only a small part of either line of ascent. Knowledge and being need to develop in reasonably close harmony. Be patient. Think of your meditation course as enrichment for every other part of your life. Wise use of your tutor will hasten the process and provide you access to someone who has traveled this way.

I was once given this kind of insight. *Think on this:* The glyph of Aquarius, two parallel lines, represents two levels of mind that, though separate, are to become one. The higher is the Real; the lower is the unreal. Those who relate to the lower may desire the higher or deny its presence, but if this represents high consciousness, those who become wise will realize the right relationship, leap over the abyss, and learn to live on two levels, not one. Life reveals its dimensions everywhere. (This is an example of a droplet received in seed-thought work.)

Seed thoughts are keys with which many doors may be opened. They key us into a vein of thought related to the word or words we choose. We can create our own seed thoughts, perhaps using words from scripture, axioms, or sayings with multi-dimensional meanings, such as, "Not my will but thine be done." However, we need to be aware, seed thoughts are never personal, for personality life does not exist at that level. They are impersonal tools that need to be in the language of the soul. Should we choose a personal thought, such as, "I would take a wise step in my life," the personal pronouns "I" and "my" bring us back to personality level. Passive meditation techniques are usually designed to provide personality level with guidance. Active meditation is designed to access soul knowledge. Furthermore, be aware we are utilizing the vibration of the seed thought or the law of attraction: *like attracts like.* We are aligning or attuning to the mind of God. *What we think upon, we become.* A wonderful tool!

The purpose of seed-thought meditation is to train our minds to pierce the veil between concrete, or rational, mind and the developing abstract levels. In practicing seed-thought (active) meditation, we also begin to make the mental mechanism magnetic in order to attract related ideas from the reservoir we have spoken of as the Cloud of Knowable Things. Alice Bailey calls this a "raincloud"—a mystical term. An older term is "Cloud of **Un**knowable." The modern occult term, "Cloud of Knowable Things," changes our conscious awareness, and we begin to believe, "I can, I can."

The combination of conscious focusing and receptive attention permits mental impressions stimulated by and related to the seed thought to register. As consciousness expands, the magnetized single thought draws to itself similar ideas of the same vibrational frequency. Spiritual law states that on non-physical levels, like attracts like. Perceptions, concepts, and realizations take shape, and precipitation-like droplets form that descend to the awaiting mental mechanism. The passive mind, already trained to wait patiently, catches the droplet—a word, thought, or symbol. This condensation of the ethers of higher mind, or vibrations from Divine Mind, is considered inspiration or impressions from God.

So we take a seed thought—"Restore the Plan on Earth," "I and the Father are one," or "Expectancy"—any will do. Though it appears to be personal, the phrase "I am" is not because it will lift us into the "I am that I am." Phrases of spiritual thought are excellent because they are charged with the power of corresponding vibration. "It is not enough to cease to do evil, it is time to do good" (Buddha). The list of possibilities is endless.

Seed-thought work usually is called *active* because we must be focused and attentive or nothing happens. Image that you are 1) focusing your will and 2) piercing a veil to connect with the spiritual essence of the word. Each word is dehydrated thought. In lifting the word to this essence, we discover the spirit behind the form in order to comprehend more fully the meaning of our seed thought. For example, *Thou shall not kill.* The physical meaning is translated to "kill a human being." Contemplating this as a seed thought, we expand our understanding to see this as *not to kill the spirit* of an individual nor to damage another in such a way that the soul cannot express in this life.

To comprehend a word's greater meaning, an ancient kabalistic way of contemplation suggests that each word contains its sum of meaning in its letters, i.e., faith—**F**inding **A**nswers **I**n **T**he **H**eart. Through acronyms, kabalists and others attempted to impart an awareness of the expanded meaning. One I coined that speaks to me is sin—**S**elf-**I**nflicted **N**onsense. This is not to make light of the subject, but to understand how we initiate experiences usually considered "sinful" to learn more about an aspect of life perhaps offensive to everyone but us.

> I recognize, of course, that evil—like Love or God or Truth—is too large to submit to any single adequate definition. But one of the better definitions for evil is that it is "militant ignorance." Militant unconsciousness.
> —M. Scott Peck, *Further Along the Road Less Traveled*[1]

Let us review how the technique works. The focused mind becomes an antenna. We lift our focus, holding it in the field of mind-stuff, in an abstract mental plane. Then, charged by the magnetic pull of the seed thought, we attract thoughts of the same essence. When finished, we shift the mind again Earthward. The impress of higher mind now vibrates in our mental makeup and will continue to do so for a time. We realize we are in an altered state, perhaps even "spacy," until we refocus on the physical world about us. For a time, we retain an expanded comprehension or increased sense of higher reality, an important part of meditation. We are magnifying our oneness with higher mind and inviting "something" to register upon us. Sitting in the silence, we often achieve that expanded sensation. Seed-thought work focuses the mind into an active, explorative mode. We concentrate on a thought, lift our mechanism to the higher part of the mental plane, by-passing the astral dimension; with our magnetized consciousness, we attract additional thoughts vibrating at that frequency. Thus, we acknowledge the importance of the thoughts we use. We allow our mind to become attuned to and taught by a wiser one.

Of course, while this is only one method of meditation, it is a major way to expand our mental mechanism because it attracts higher ethers and organizes them for the mental body. Let us describe the mental body with its distinctive levels of mind, as taught in ageless wisdom.

	Key Word
Divine contemplations directed to humanity	**Contemplation**
Inspiration: holiness, beauty, encouragement	**Inspiration**
Cloud of Knowable Things: intuition, inventiveness, great wisdom	**Cloud of Knowable Things**
High Self * Solar Angel: the thinker; insight and vision	**High Self * Solar Angel**
Conscious mind: thoughtforms—personal and others	**Thoughtforms**
Programming, illusions, and glamours relating to self-image: ideas of sexual and material gratification and of separateness	**Self-image**
Inherited patterns of thinking: subconscious present and past; old karma carried forward, instinctual	**Patterns, Tapes**

Figure 16. The Mental Plane (from highest vibration to lowest).

As we have noted, the first work of meditation is known as "building the cup," a receptacle in which to capture the impressions we will receive. Passive meditation builds that cup. Receptiveness, quiet periods of sitting, guided imagery, and listening within encourage the process. We begin to become conscious of impressions, whether feeling, auditory, or visual. We build the mechanism for registering that with which we connect. Our efforts begin in the conscious mind, and we prepare the cup to receive the droplets that will fall from above. Thoughtforms, ever present in the mind of God, densify and collect in response to empowered seed thoughts. They rain down as droplets into the cup, the conscious mind ready and receptive. The structure of our mental body is strengthened.

It is most advantageous to master passive meditation prior to beginning active meditation, the next step to expansion of consciousness for this contemporary stage of humanity.

Time after time, we focus new energy, cause precipitation, and capture the droplets in our cup. This densified soul substance, usually called "fiery," affects our spiritualized and evolving etheric body according to the condition for which we are ready; transmutation thus can occur. As the focused mind draws similar frequencies—related in vibration, thought, and nature—from what is called the mind-stuff, or substance of the mental plane, the meditator is forming next level of mind. Bit by bit, we realize expansion of consciousness. Contemplation then helps us organize the mind-stuff we have drawn to ourselves. New ideas become grounded in our awareness. We come to know, and the organized mind-stuff builds an accumulation of mental mechanism. As our mental body develops level by level, we are challenged to live our new awareness, to "walk our talk."

We may need to be reminded, all of this has two purposes: first, the advancement of our own spiritual growth; second, the advancement of human evolution. Each of us, a cell in the consciousness of the whole, contributes to the human group mind even as we prepare individually for a leap forward to enter the kingdom of souls. As we invoke the light to guide us on our path, it illuminates others as well. Those capable of soul consciousness will serve to guide humanity's advancement.

As we have learned from ancient wisdom teachings, humanity's goal is soul infusion, just as is our personal goal. Soul infusion is considered the third initiation in the esoteric Christian tradition. Each of us in our sojourn through the human kingdom must align with the soul to fulfill our reason for incarnation.

The active work of focusing stimulates the experience of response, being taught by Divine Mind more profoundly than is possible with passive meditation. As the term "passive" indicates, we wait and accept; on the other hand, active implies action: the active meditator stands at the door and knocks. Indeed, we need to know both techniques and to learn which is more likely to achieve specific objectives.

*Spirituality has to do
with the ethics of
applying our knowledge.*

When we use the focusing technique in active meditation, we are tightening our mental perception, as if we were positioning a magnifying glass to concentrate sunlight to ignite a flame. We begin by repeating the seed thought, much like a mantra. Gradually, we connect with the rush of energy that lifts our mind into the impersonal abstract level. Holding the seed thought, yet keeping the cup available to be filled with additional related thoughts, we seek to capture the incoming impressions.

As our attentive mind receives the inspired thoughts that rush in, the mind mechanism is held open and attentive to the subtle touches. At this point we begin to write as we capture incoming thoughts, not evaluating, simply allowing the flow to move into the mind and through it to the hand and onto the paper. Indeed the hand is merely an extension of the mind. The work is to be open, peacefully poised, and allow the precipitated thoughts to rain into the cup, to ripple into the awaiting mechanism. The writing is to secure these thoughts—often profound, poetic, and inspiring. We may experience without capturing the sweet nectar, but to capture it is our reward. This experience is called "taught by God" or "accessing the information from behind the veil."

Helen Keller lived without sight and sound in a world that eluded her. When her tutor Anne Sullivan at last awakened her, it was not to the outer light—she remained as blind as ever—but to the inner light. When she comprehended a new reality, the process of humanizing development within her could begin.

So it is with us. Until we awaken to the soul, our physical senses hold us in the limited sensory world, blind to the real. When the light of the soul comes on, we awaken to a new dimension of knowing, feeling, and loving. Until such time, we can only long for these.

Until we experience this shift ourselves, we only hear tales of trail blazers who have traveled into the unknown and returned to share their experiences. Made new by this inner light, they gain access to the light of consciousness that will illuminate the entire human kingdom in due time. The enlightened evoke in us a great desire to adventure as they have into a grand reality, surpassing what we now only crudely sense.

At personality level we remind ourselves,
I am the Soul.
>*I am not the body;*
>>*I am not the emotions;*
>>>*I am not the mind.*

>>*I am the user of the body;*
>>>*I am the user of the emotions;*
>>>>*I am the user of the mind.*
I am the Soul.

We develop a higher perspective, and we dedicate ourselves to expansion of consciousness. A new point of reference emerges as we focus the power of personality in allegiance to the soul. We align the levels of personality to work in conjunction with the soul and its purpose. As we learn focusing techniques, we discover our will and how to use it wisely. Remember, will is the "power" part of the expression, "light, love, and power." We seek light to perceive, love (Lots Of Vital Energy), and will (power) under the guidance of soul consciousness.

We continue to learn how to cooperate in the use of our will through seed-thought work. We learn to keep our minds alert and focused in a desired direction, resolving not to slip into mind-wandering, daydreaming, or problem-solving. As we implement such practices, other valuable powers of mind awake and become known to us.

Each path selects the concepts it considers most important for enhancing meditation. While some are quite abstract, others are concrete and specific. Seed thoughts may be single words, statements, mantras, paragraphs, koans (paradoxes), questions, Bible verses, the names of God. They may be identified as precepts, realizations, qualities, attributes, themes, or virtues. Some paths have a large number of these (more than 100); others have few. Methods using seed thoughts stress the importance of meditation upon each thought for a period of time (generally for a number of times or days or perhaps years) in order to penetrate beyond its common form to its inner reality. Some systems use objects as a focus of attention; others stress neither seed thoughts nor objects as meditative devices.

We are already familiar with guided imagery. Seed-thought work is in the natural progression of our studies after we have learned to relax and to center and have had some experience with passive meditation. Our first step was to "build the cup." As we do this, we grow in our ability to follow guided meditation at a deep level. The receptivity gained creates a consciousness into which thoughts flow. We begin to retain our impressions and bring them back. This indicates the cup is formed. We now capture the rush of thoughts that shower upon us during active meditation. We realize we are being taught from a non-physical level of consciousness, designated as connecting with ideas contained in the soul.

Agni Yoga Wisdom

In our seed-thought work we will use the themes and virtues of the Agni path to self-actualization. As we have noted, Agni Yoga, a modern approach, is to aid the process of synthesis through purity of thought, emotion, and physical lifestyle. We try to improve all of these and blend truths into a pattern for daily living. A virtuous life is sought by deriving inspiration for direction from themes, rather than conforming to rigid rules, doctrine, or dogma. We synthesize these themes day by day as best we can, each of us proceeding at his or her own pace and led from within.

Earlier, we reviewed the idea of being-ness versus knowledge. By focusing on these seed thoughts, we pursue a desired quality or virtue. We add to the line of being as well as the line of knowledge—for both are attuning to the quality—that we might comprehend it in its fullness, but we do so repeatedly because, as we have learned, *what we focus upon, we become.* As we live our themes, they become a part of our line of being, not just our line of knowledge.

We have chosen Agni Yoga themes and virtues for several reasons. The Agni way is open to everyone; it is timely to the new Aquarian age and the quest for greater knowledge, without regard to background or nature—scientific or devotional. This modern path synthesizes the spiritual work of recent history and teaches humanity to build aspects of the self that transmute human nature to reflect the One Light that illuminates all life. Neither Eastern nor Western, it encompasses both and unifies our personal inner and outer realities.

This era we call the Aquarian Age, the Maya refer to as the *Age of Flowers.* This ancient tradition and others believe our higher energy centers are to bloom in this period and emanate their fragrance/essence/awareness to the world. The universal message is that the time has come to realize love-caring is an aspect of spirituality. In fact, the injunction, "Thou shall not judge," reminds us we are seeking to create a path toward higher consciousness by living love.

Yoga means "union." In Matthew 11.29, Jesus said, "Take my yoke upon you." Both "yoke" and "yoga" come from *yug,* a Sanskrit word meaning "union." It seems Master Jesus was saying his yoga, his way of union with God, was different—not a teaching of the preceding period of law, *an eye for an eye,* but a way of love for all to practice. In Matthew 5.17, he said he did *not come to "weaken" the law but to fulfill it.* In this yoga of Christ, we seek to yoke heart and mind through meditation, learning to love and to serve.

Another thought important to the yoga of the Christ is to understand that his words "my burden is light" do not mean "without weight" but that en*light*enment is the goal of his union/ yoga. Christianity only rarely perceives itself as a path of enlighten- ment, one of many valuable secrets Esoteric Christianity offers.

We would also realize in Matthew 11.28-30, this yoga was different from the "law" teachings of the previous era. Here concepts of love are new. Christianity's mission is to lift its disciples from solar plexus understanding—judgment, right or wrong, good or bad—to the heart center. We are challenged in the Way of the Christ to learn about love as a path to God and, in fact, to enter into love and service in ways often uncomfortable to the ego level of personality.

In these lessons we identify twenty-five major seed thoughts. Nine themes and twelve virtues of Agni Yoga are embodied in this modern path of synthesis, compatible with both Christianity and Kabalah. Four more are added: "expansion" (to enhance our comprehension of "beginning"), "I am the soul," "compassion," and "illumination" (important to all meditation mastery). We seek to comprehend the expanded meanings of the words so we may contact new awareness and allow their impact to register.

Since it is important to use each seed thought several times, we suggest you consider a lesson incomplete until you have meditated as instructed over a period of days. You may choose to meditate daily, or, due to circumstances, you may take longer to fulfill the minimum. If possible, complete each session within one month. If meditations are extended over a very long period, the momentum is lost and relatively superficial experiences may result.

Today many students are enthusiastic about just such a psycho-spiritual path as we are presenting. Modern spiritual disciples eagerly embrace an ecumenical and transformational esoteric practice. In this time of renewed interest in spiritual technologies, this contemporary yoga continues to emerge, so we focus upon Agni themes and virtues, invoking their power as we practice soul-infusion techniques. You will find it exciting to participate in this new and evolutionary yoga.

Not yet a clearly defined process, the Agni path continues to reveal itself as humanity builds communication capabilities with the soul, individually and collectively. In this synthesis, we integrate heart and mind. New levels of the mental body form in the individual and in the collective, and we begin to realize that our meditations have a greater effect than anticipated. We understand we are doing an evolutionary work, that our meditations bless both ourselves and humanity. Indeed, our meditation is a service we render even as we seek enlightenment/salvation. Our word "salvation" comes from the Latin *salvus,* which means "safe," or "to save." When you see the word "salvation," teach yourself, "salvation = enlightenment." This affirms the truth and reconciles the wording of the Western and Eastern paths.

Agni, meaning "fire," reminds us of the fervor of all who seek God. Light and fire have been used throughout the ages by saints and sages to speak of the divine presence. Thus this path links us to all spiritual seekers. As a symbol, fire is familiar to Christians as tongues of fire over the heads of the apostles on Pentecost. We recall the burning bush of Moses, the flames around the dancing Shiva, and the importance of fire and flame in Native American rituals. Zoroastrians used the simple flame, nothing else, as their symbol of divinity.[2]

Issues of purification often are spoken of as "turning up the flame." We seek to comprehend the concept of the flame and the light. We light the fire consciously, but our tolerance in the purification process determines how rapidly the smoke gives way to the light. We bring to consciousness many qualities and abilities hidden deep within. In the process of rediscovering and integrating these, we synthesize spirit and matter, past and present, independence and interdependence.

Even when we refuse to look consciously at distressing situations in our lives, the unconscious influence of our dedication to a meditation practice helps us mature. Eventually we begin to stabilize by building a purified and personalized point of higher consciousness; from there we perceive the purpose of our lives more clearly. We learn how to cooperate more easily with life, the great teacher. Such conscious work empowers us to grow into the predestined learning the soul pursues. Aspiration grows and empowers us as we connect with soul energies, whether all registers consciously or not.

Mind Screen and the Importance of Visualization

As we learn to use our imagination (image-making ability), we cast pictures (images) upon the screen we are building in the mind, and they register in such a way that we perceive the image. We call this a "mind screen" to designate its inward nature. As we develop this image-making capability, dreams are enhanced, thoughtforms appear more real, and we develop more visual approaches to learning. The mind screen thus serves well the personality that has developed this capability. Once in place, the higher consciousness also casts images upon the screen as impressions, pictures, symbols, and scenes.

The ability to visualize opens us to the messages of both the subconscious and the High Self so that visualization and exercises to enhance visualization are more important than we may have thought.

Visualization techniques can make many otherwise elusive areas more available: ego states, sub-personalities, spirit beings, past-life experiences, inner conflicts, and inner resources. Visualization experiences can unfold in the psyche while in the altered state as real—to be felt, understood, and reconciled. Information received can be brought more easily into the present moment. Children, especially the very young, are in an easily accessed state such as this much of the time, though unconsciously. As attachment to the material plane develops, this once easily accessed state is often lost and adults generally must make some effort to enter into it again.

Envisioning, however, is a different process. It consists of the practice of bringing into focus the part of the Plan we do perceive. Like a forest, the vision appears to be brimming with wholeness. Just as each tree has its unique characteristics, little noticed when we see the entire forest, so do we. Like the trees of the forest, we contribute our part to the whole, even while having our personal struggles. While we comprehend the whole, we then shift to focus on our own segment. We see and affirm our part of the Plan, however we understand it, energizing the part we perceive. Then we replace our part back into the symbol we use for humanity's Plan. We envision the whole and our segment to bring both into outer form. Envisioning is sustaining the whole of what we perceive, while energizing our piece, but understanding the importance of both.

We could say, then, envisioning is attuning to the set of blueprints in the ethers given by higher intelligences, utilizing the creative force of the divine architect, the God-Within. Over and over, we attune our mind (receiver set) to the higher broadcast,

God-Transcendent, until it can stay "on beam" (concentration). Then the creative within begins to step down the higher picture. This process, envisioning, helps us manifest that which we have recognized.

The Active Meditation Technique

Let us use our chosen seed thought. What are we going to do? First, think, "The seed thought for today is _____." Now see the word(s) written as if on a billboard. Observe it, then begin to say it over and over to yourself. As you do this, it becomes a mantra for you. It is filling your mind. (Even if you are not accustomed to envisioning, attempt to see it anyway.) Hear it, and say it. This concentration of personal attention creates a focus, gathers your senses, and helps you become increasingly aware of the word(s), its frequency, and its quality.

Next, note the vibration of the word or phrase (it may be called "the quality," if you prefer). Feel its energy, its emotional charge. Is it exciting, strong, soft, pulsating, fluid, or intense? Note the energy you sense as you are filled with the vibration of the seed thought. Your feeling sense assists you. Those more visual may see pictures, but that is not the goal. At this step you are to sense vibration, cadence, rhythm, etc., a total sensory experience of the seed thought. The difference between "getting pictures" and sensing the quality may be thought of as the difference between watching a movie of a thunderstorm and actually being present in the intensity of a storm.

The next step is to press against the thought, to penetrate it, to become one with it as it fills your mind. Continue to see and say the word or phrase, and allow yourself to be drawn to a particular part of the phrase, one or two words perhaps. If the seed thought is one word, you may find it seems to break down. "Transformation" may be broken down into thoughts such as "trans," "form," "creation," or a phrase like, "The higher self guides the unfolding life," becomes "higher self," "self guides," or "unfolding life."

After you have proceeded to think along a "thread of awareness," you may find your mind darting into other areas. If it wanders too far from the "seed," bring yourself back, and restate the seed thought. Simply refocus your attention. Say the seed thought to yourself again, and gently begin the process once again, as though you were prompting a young child.

Say the seed thought, feel it, and capture the related insights. Again, jot down your thoughts while keeping your mind focused and your sense of connection. Return to the seed thought a number of times until you feel you have done enough for one session. Then rest. If a kind of "high" follows from the rush of energy you have contacted, think of this as a gift or blessing received for your dedicated effort. Enjoy.

Basic Procedures

We will soon go through an entire seed-thought procedure. Throughout this course, we will continue to use the same basic process with gradual changes at subsequent stages. While similar to other methods, the differences in this procedure make it dynamic and vigorous. The power of the mind penetrates the inner significance of a seed thought as we contact our superconscious, or higher mind. This effort is a subtle combination of steadily focused thought and an openness to accept realizations that come—not by willful forcing. Learning from a seed thought requires relaxed alertness and persistent but untroubled concentration.

Using the concept of "in the light of the soul," we affirm that we live under the watchful eye of our spiritual self, the soul. With soul-infusion techniques we visualize the soulstar overhead, acknowledging and drawing upon the soul as an available and viable energy source. If this idea is new to you, consider it in this way:

Personality is a projection of the soul, an aspect of the soul created and projected into the denser reality to assist the soul in gathering information and experiences through which it matures. Therefore, personality is like a child or an idea, a creation of the soul in that the soul is the life-energy source. In our meditations we will always acknowledge the soulstar as the "light of the soul" energizing the experience of the personality self. Here we visualize (give form to the concept) the soulstar, a bountiful quantity of light, love, and power readily available to personality for its use.

Imagine personality as a deep-sea diver experiencing in a darker, slower, and heavier environment than soul does. Personality clings to its lifeline—like a silver cord, or a breath of life. Living at a lower vibrational level, in the murky waters of muddy pools with its roots in the slower vibrations, personality sends lovely shoots of greenery upward—healing thoughts, refining, caring, seeking—developing its unique self as it comes to fruition. Remember, *ye are Gods,* destined to bloom and grow in ways wondrous to behold.

> The Son of God became human in order that humans might become Gods and become children of God.
> —Thomas Aquinas, *Compendium Theologiae*

I would like to share that once upon a time, my friend and mentor, Torkom Saraydarian, gave me two seed thoughts to use, each one for three to six months. It can be done by overcoming boredom and really penetrating into deeper levels of the thought. That in itself is a good discipline for the aspiring spiritual student. A fresh welling up seemed to occur after each dry period. I was amazed at how much may be realized with persistence.

Let Us Review

In seed-thought work we consciously focus upon the form(s) created by the word or phrase; then we pierce the form in successive stages to discover the essence behind the word itself. Questions may be useful in directing this process, but if you function effectively without them, do not feel compelled to use them every time you meditate.

Procedure for Seed-Thought Meditation

1. Begin to relax with several natural breaths, singing softly or chanting.

2. Read a brief piece of devotional material.

3. Close your eyes, and turn your attention within. Use your opening gesture: select a bow, the sign of the cross, hands in prayer position (as you choose, but do adopt a gesture). Become still, and continue to relax.

4.   Now visualize a point of clear, white light ten inches or so above your head—the soulstar, light of the soul. Focus upon this vibrating light, and cause it to expand its radiance, remaining clear and bright.

5.   Draw the soulstar energy down to your heart. Magnify your feelings of love-caring. Allow love to flow. Feel it move through your emotional nature—clearing, cleansing, nurturing. Consciously bless the body. Feel love for it. This love and nurturing flows through the emotional nature and the body, healing past hurts, forgiving, and neutralizing all negativity. Fill yourself with the positive energy of the soulstar. Begin to radiate that love throughout your body; then emanate it into the space around you.

6.   Now move your attention to the mind. Seek to lift your focus from personality mind to interact with Higher Mind. We guide this shift by taking a breath and thinking, "I would be lifted from limited mind to Divine Mind."

7.   By focused intent and active will, we form a straight line of light to pierce the veil that separates the higher from the lower.

8.   Lift your magnetized consciousness into the Cloud of Knowable Things.

9.   Now imagine a line of light from the roof of the mouth upward and extending through and about ten inches beyond the forehead. If you feel with your finger just above the hairline, a tender place or slight indentation indicates a sensitive point. We draw this imaginary line of light from this point—arms extended in front, palms together, lift your arms to either side of your head at the temples, making the unicorn horn of ancient legend. (Normally you will not need to lift your hands and arms in such a way, but do it once to be aware of the WILL involved and the power needed to create this focus.) With purity of mind, we form a magnetized consciousness by focusing on the seed thought, lifting, and magnetizing it by the power of the heart. When lifted into the Cloud of Knowable Things, this magnetized line of light precipitates droplets. Just as moisture collects and drops begin to fall when climatic conditions are just right, we are creating "precipitation."

10.   Begin to draw to you that which you need. Ask to perceive, intuit, and know. Ask the great questions of the aspirant:

- How do I find my part in the mandala of human endeavors?
- How may I serve the higher cause?
- What is mine to do? What part of this is mine to do this day?

11.   Using the technique of acting "as if," perceive yourself as a soul-infused personality, and focus upon your seed thought. _____ (Insert your thought here.)

12.   Now bring the subtle impressions back to the conscious mind, for we would bring the passion of our heart and mind together within the chalice of our own being. To capture the thoughts you have contacted, jot down the phrases, ideas, concepts, or insights that come—also any symbols, designs, or forms that enter your mind. Mentally ask questions of these impressions, knowing responses will come.

13.   Speaking as a soul-infused personality, say the Great Invocation (see Appendix), both as a service and as a way of expressing thankfulness for all you have received.

14.   Conclude this work by speaking the sacred tone, *Om,* aloud three times, and use your closing gesture.

Send your responses or questions about lesson content or procedures to the mentors, share reactions or meaningful experiences, or tell us of any problems we may help with. If you have not enrolled, you may do so now.

Assignment

Seed Thought: Compassion

While compassion is not a theme or virtue in the Agni teachings, it is our goal. Compassion is the result of the integration of heart and mind or, we might say, the realization of love-wisdom. It is said the true purpose of planetary consciousness is to express compassion, and hidden deep within each of us is the divine nature that can reflect compassion. The goddess Kuan Yin, divine mother of the East, is called the Bodhisattva of Compassion. Certainly we think of Mary, mother of Jesus, as compassionate, and St. Francis of Assisi, Albert Schweitzer, and Mother Teresa—wonderful role models as we create and expand our own compassion. We hold in mind,

There is equality, there is justice where there is compassion. Compassion implies intelligence. When there is that marvelous flame of compassion then there is no difference between the poor and the rich, between the well placed and those people who have nothing on God's Earth . . . . Let us find out if we can become compassionate. To come to that point one must be extraordinarily alert to all human frailties, to all human limitations, which are one's own limitations. You are not separate from the rest of mankind. If once you see the truth of that, then your whole attitude towards life and action changes completely.

—Jiddu Krishnamurti
The World of Peace (Meetings at Brockwood Park)

To Live As a Soul

More than once when I sat all alone,
the mortal limit of the Self was loosed,
and passed into the nameless,
as a cloud melts into heaven.

—Alfred, Lord Tennyson

M ost Christians grow up indoctrinated to the concept of having a soul. When we accept the concept that *I am the Soul,* a major shift occurs. We have a certain orientation to life if we consider ourselves a human *with* a soul; if we consider ourselves a *soul* undergoing a human experience, we will have quite another.

Affirmation of the Disciple

I am a point of light within a greater Light.
I am a strand of loving energy within the stream of Love divine.
I am a point of Sacrificial Fire,
    focused within the fiery Will of God.
        And thus I stand.
I am a way by which men may achieve.
I am a source of strength, enabling them to stand.
I am a beam of light, shining upon their way.
        And thus I stand.

And standing thus revolve
And tread this way the ways of men,
And know the ways of God.
    And thus I stand.

Esoteric teachings provide a model of God as the Great Creator, both masculine and feminine in nature, separated into individually distinct units and sent forth into creation to experience and return. This spark of fiery consciousness is called a *monad* (meaning "the One"); as it frequents the highest planes to experience life in greater density, it projects a soul. The soul in turn puts down a personality through which to experience physical, astral, and mental realms. This process of descent is known as the path of involution; the path of return, or evolution, is the ascent upward from matter.

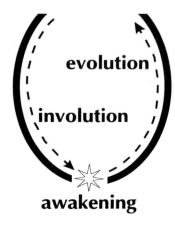

Figure 17. Through Involution to Evolution.

Relationships provide the major method of growth for humanity. Thus souls mature through interaction with one another. They will blossom when awareness eventually reaches a level of understanding where they begin to take an active known part in the Plan. It must be remembered that each monad left its source with the same potential; the small flame has the same properties as the entire fire.

The monad is given the seed of the entire Plan, as well as its own particular pattern to complete. The mature soul vibrates to the Plan and, after completing the human path of initiation, moves eventually to solar initiations. From there, we experience the cosmic initiations of which we now know nothing. Even further into the future, the soul will surrender all its gifts and treasures to monad, and the monad will return them to the Source. The prodigal daughter/son completes the journey.

In Esoteric Christianity we learn to conceive of ourselves as souls evolving through personal experience toward maturity. We strive to be wise in the ways of the soul—seeing with the eyes of the soul, knowing what the soul knows. Listening (passive meditation) attunes us to the soul frequency, and meditation builds the cup in which we will capture the droplets of soul consciousness that come.

To become the soul, the "I am," it must be real to us. We have misidentified with personality all of our lives, believing we were merely the body, the talent, the outer rather than the inner. Only as we deepen our spiritual life do we begin to correct this error. Now we make a concentrated effort to claim our true identity.

Spiritual Technologies

The incoming mental energy of the Aquarian age pushes us to utilize wisely all the insights we have acquired. The prompting of our time is to move us from intellect to intuition. The more we use the powers of mind and the more we experiment, the more we will find—rather, rediscover—keys to the nonphysical reality that is the true Self. Step by step we move experientially from intellect, as we have believed in it, to new realities we now intuit. We already have keys to unlock capabilities greater than we now use. We lay a foundation for future discoveries through the use of spiritual technology (how-to's) to link our conscious mind and spiritual self in a coworking relationship.

The desired shift and most important work of all spiritual technology is to know our true nature. From ancient times, wisdom teachings have included methods and exercises—technology for change. Procedures and language have differed, according to people and culture. Techniques and their purposes have been veiled so the untrained could not comprehend what was to be achieved or realized. In the oral tradition individual teachers, gurus, and mentors used discretion in the dissemination of their wisdom. The degree of commitment, as well as the personal spiritual maturity of each candidate, determined the directions given. Little has changed today, except the proliferation of written materials and the higher level of academic education in the general population permit the reading, not always the comprehension, of mystery teachings. "Blinds" are no longer possible.

We are calling these methods of assisting seekers "spiritual technology." To serve well an intimate relationship requires the integrity of both teacher and student. Committed to nurturing the student, the teacher must keep in mind the divine potential awaiting release—i.e., holding the immaculate conception for another—and carefully monitor the supporting checks and balances needed for change to manifest. When we begin to awaken, we discover the self long veiled by personality. Indeed, here we touch into archetypal energies. Impersonality has a new value, and both student and teacher are performing from more than their lesser selves.

The correct match of student and mentor therefore becomes increasingly important. A given type of mentor, not necessarily a particular teacher, may be necessary for progress to occur. Or a certain type of student may have to balance energies, karma, or experience with one mentor before moving on to another. Each personality must subside, and each soul must wisely impart its gift to the other.

It has been said that soon after awakening, we will be placed in the hands of a mentor for disciplining our will. This may be brought about by either checking or stimulating will, whichever is needed to define or shape our pattern.

We are reminded time and time again, "When the student is ready, the teacher appears." Both student and teacher must attune to the roles they play to comprehend the significance of the relationship. We might consider: is it karmic or cosmic that our souls touch? *Meditation guides us toward our veiled identity.*

Our Feeling (Astral) Nature

Knowing that humanity shares a common physical reality with only a small portion (the body) personally our own, we must understand we have a similar challenge to grasp our own feeling (astral) nature. Since we all share a common astral dimension, even though we each have our own rather clearly defined astral body, it is easily invaded by the potent rushes contacted in the sea of astral energy in which each individual feeling nature swims. Thus we are constantly clearing our private astral portion, caring for it just as we wash and care for our physical body.

Comprehending that we share a common astral reality with only a small portion defined as our own helps us understand why we pick up the feelings and vibrations of our neighbors so easily. The sensitivity of the astral nature focused through the etheric body provided instinctual knowing and survival skills for humanity long before it achieved individuation some 18 million years ago, according to ageless wisdom teachings. Since then, that astral nature has served to attune us to the feeling nature of those about us, reinforcing our understanding on an instinctual level through unspoken communication.

Like fish swimming in an aquarium, humanity goes about its business of living, perceiving its direction largely from this astral level. Even as this is said, we should realize we have—thank goodness—the assistance of a veil, as it is called, to hold back a large portion of the vast reservoir of astral energy. This filter has held the most acute accumulated emotions of humanity's past in abeyance, protecting us individually and the evolving group from being overwhelmed by torrents of raw emotion engraved upon the astral reflective ethers on the involution arc.

With consciousness continuing to evolve, we are told the time has come for humanity to assume the task of clearing and cleansing these astral imprints, neutralizing by conscious design the age-old feelings of hostility, hatred, rage, and savagery that have created a miasma of dark, or lower, vibrations around our planet.

Since all of us share this common area, we also share the responsibility of purification. Though we work on our emotional nature, establish a degree of serenity, and enjoy this for a brief time, we soon find we are absorbing pollutants once again from the surrounding ethers. Day by day, we continue the effort of clearing, centering, uplifting, and realigning this tender feeling nature to the creative love of the higher frequencies. By such daily service, we keep ourselves in a positive state of heart, feeling, and sensitivity. As we advance in the opening of the chakras, located in the etheric body, we advance in our ability to draw subtler (higher frequency) energy from the astral plane into ourselves to help our portion of the astral nature remain in a more positive state of consciousness.

We recall that the lower three chakras, or centers of conscious-ness, are well developed in all humanity incarnating at this time. Thus we look to the development of higher centers, our divine perspectives, to assist us in bringing our divine sensitivities into activity. As this higher consciousness occurs, rapid clearing of the cruel, destructive past should ensue. Indeed, this is the positive energy needed ". . . to seal the door where evil dwells," as referred to in the Great Invocation.

The energy centers, or chakras, may be viewed as terminals that enable the energies of the soul to be stepped up or down. Each center coordinates the exchange of specific energies according to the pattern held for an individual personality (i.e., karmic seeds). The lower centers in all individuals deal with activities in the realm of bioenergetics and instinctual life. As the higher centers come into play, psychological, creative, and spiritual awareness is energized. As this growth continues, soul energies are invoked more and more, received, and distributed through all the centers into their activities.

The Mantra

Another tool commonly used for focusing in meditation is the mantra, a word or phrase spoken ritualistically. The popular movement of Transcendental Meditation (TM) is one approach of many based upon a mantra given to the student by a teacher, which has a centering and consciousness-altering effect. Some believe a mantra is limited to evoking a relaxation response that relieves deep stress; others believe it carries meditators to a level of spiritual vibrations. It is important to remember, words are vibrations, and affixed to thoughtforms; they affect us more than we often realize.

Some incorrectly assume a single mantra used consistently will unlock all the doors to enlightenment. However, experienced meditators recognize that we may reach higher states by using additional methods, consistent with the practice of gurus and mentors who offer new mantras to students as they ascend the ladder of spiritual development. If we examine the concept of levels in considering paradoxes, we can identify several meditation activities as useful at different times for different people. Thus, there need be no serious contradiction in instruction.

Creative moments or breakthroughs may happen at any stage of our journey and are always wonderful. When the influence of the Higher showers upon us, we feel blessed and awed. We know something splendid is occurring. While we cannot make these things happen consistently, we do encourage the process by repeatedly putting ourselves in posture as we persist in repeating "I am the Soul," inwardly and outwardly. *This becomes the guiding attitude for those who seek to know God.*

The will to receive acts as a magnet: being receptive is very important for the new condition to manifest. Too often we may believe doing the will, or our dedicated practice, *should* make *it* happen. Now we are introduced to another condition, one that is feminine but also will.

Figure 18. Will: Active and Receptive. Will (+) is push, action, creativity; yet will (-) is surrender, receptivity, willingness to allow the flow to move us. When meditating, this latter attitude trusts and waits patiently, gently allowing life to guide us to our point of destiny.

Once, in a most passionate time of fervor, striving to be all that I might be and bemoaning my lack of perfection, I was told, "One need not be perfect, but one must be willing." Since then, I have sought to be willing with greater conscientiousness.

We adopt the attitude we deem appropriate, spiritual practices we can embrace, and themes we comprehend to create a spiritual lifestyle with all the understanding we have at the moment. It takes courage to make spiritual decisions and abide by them. Lives must be adjusted daily to satisfy the needs of the hour and yet at the same time carry out service needed by humanity. It takes courage to be so futuristic on a daily basis that we demonstrate continually how responding to the world challenge is more important than the petty concerns of personality.

What a challenge this presents. But the transformation power of all aspirants rests in cultivating the attitude of the *silent watcher: to clear away the currents of the moment and the confusion those currents bring and still stay in touch with the vibration of the soul.

In the East one hears of the "sound current" or "silent sound." Think of this as *the heartbeat of the soul that personality hears in the silence*. Once heard, it may be lost, so we endeavor time and time again to reattune to it. Unnecessary speech and negative words affect us, as do offensive music and noise. We become increasingly sensitive to what obscures the "heartbeat" and what aids us in hearing it.

Loving-understanding in so many simple areas of life assists us in making our life sacred. We release the obstructions and cultivate the consciousness of soul to the degree we are able to perceive it. Messages from one level to the other heard telepathically also assist us in finding our way and in manifesting this quality. We perceive ourselves as belonging to the group of world servers and participate in the work at hand. We focus on the highest consciousness to which we can vibrate, and as we do so, it is stepped down to humanity's outer life. Meditation is to the spirit as physical food is to the body.

Steps Facilitate the Meditation Process

Four basic steps (form, quality, purpose, cause) in the seed-thought procedure provide a process of exploration to guide but not restrict us. If you are able to penetrate into the essence of the seed thought without them, do so. If they are useful at the beginning but then seem to limit your penetration, follow your own lead. You do not need to receive answers at each step in every session unless, of course, you find this helpful.

Remember, seed-thought meditation is to experience the essence and expand the comprehension of the thought. We use the thought to experience other ideas that vibrate to it. The keynote of the thought registers a frequency and, by sounding the word or vibrating the keynote, we attract additional related words, ideas, or concepts on the same frequency. Our goal: to gain access to all the seed thought contains.

In experiencing the word(s), we consider that form, quality (emotion), purpose, and cause advance us into the abstract levels of mind where the subtler levels of the seed thoughts are contained. The steps will be helpful when we have difficulty penetrating the subtler meanings or essence of a word(s). (The steps are designed in the following format so that the reader may photostat or cut it out for a bookmark.)

We move deeper into the experience of the word as the process is used. As you explore a seed thought, perceive yourself as an open, expanded, and sensitive mind. Lift your mind, and press it into the all-pervading mind of God. Imagine you are seeking to be taught by this knowable contact. The aim of active forms of meditation is to bring abstract ideas captured as seeds into more concrete form for understanding and dynamic use in daily life.

When you have done all you can, relax; draw your mind back, imprinted with new knowing. Having perceived new information, designs, or impressions, relax and allow them to integrate. They may linger; enjoy reverberating in the afterglow of your altered mental state, a good time for both vulnerability and high creativity.

> O God, make me as a hollow reed from which the pith of Seth hath been blown, that I may become a clear channel through which thy Love may flow to others.
>
> —A Bahai prayer

As you press into the steps, say or think them slowly: form, quality, purpose, cause. You will often realize you are being drawn more than you are pressing. Hold your mind focused, and the creative action will draw you to it.

As we have learned from ancient wisdom teachings, again, *we become what we focus upon*—the most important reason we repeat certain words or seed thoughts time and again in meditation. If we hold "love" in our minds and become attuned to the word, we penetrate its essence. We become one with the thoughtform, its reason for being, and its relationship to the

---

Stepping Inward through Seed-Thought Meditation

Form. This refers to the form of the word or words. Example: grace. The letters create a form; saying the word over and over causes it to become another kind of form, a mantra. So we work first with the visual or written form, then spoken. We begin to repeat the seed thought. Say it and attempt to visualize the word as if on a billboard to begin to feel the vibration. G-R-A-C-E.

Quality. Consider quality as the emotional charge or impulse, what the word or thought feels like. Seek to attune to the quality or vibration, the impact or the energy of the word(s) with which you are working. "Grace, grace, grace." Feel the quality—absorbing, sustaining, uplifting. Now press inwardly another step to discover the purpose.

Purpose. What is the purpose of grace? Why? Grace—why? To care for me, to uplift, to free me from limitation, to grow, to come to know—a series of thoughts. Allow them to flow, and if the mind wanders, center again upon the word. Now try to press within again.

Cause. Why? To experience God—cause. First cause: God's love is grace—healing force, life, good, clearing, help, sustenance. From cause to effect, return and know. Think, "Cause, cause, grace—cause."

183

The Great Invocation

From the point of Light
within the Mind of God
Let light stream forth
into the minds of men.
Let Light descend on Earth.

From the point of Love
within the Heart of God
Let love stream forth
into the hearts of men.
May Christ return to Earth.

From the Center where the
Will of God is known
Let purpose guide the
little wills of men—
The purpose which the
Masters know and serve.

From the center which
we call the race of men
Let the Plan of Love
and Light work out.
And may it seal the door
where evil dwells.

Let Light and Love and Power
restore the Plan on Earth.

Source of Life. As we posture ourselves and penetrate the energy (emotional charge) and form of any seed thought, we allow it to permeate our consciousness, our very nature. We expand our consciousness as we open to new ideals.

Until we find ways to identify with purifying concepts or energies by experiencing them, we cannot express qualities of higher consciousness. For example, we cannot know what "harmlessness" means until we connect with and realize the ideal. As this quality develops within us, we will see it in others. As we have all heard, we cannot recognize that which we have not experienced. Working with seed thoughts helps us focus upon what it is we would become.

Expansion of consciousness generally means building a new reference point from which to experience higher awareness or "unfolding the lotus of high consciousness." Step by step, we add to our awareness one quality or virtue after another, like the lotus petals opening. It is important to realize that growth occurs gradually. A flower bud does not fly open with the speed of a jack-in-the-box.

Although there seems no stopping point, we do reach increasingly rewarding levels. This indicates we are indeed "on the path." The process becomes so satisfying, it reduces any compulsion to "get there, to be safe at last." Such compulsive thinking comes from distorted motivation; compulsive thinking indicates a lack of trust in the universe to love and provide for us. If we try too hard, we may indeed force seeming growth, but we risk developing mental and emotional problems as well. This is a good place to remember the fable of the tortoise and the hare, both questing even as we. The steady, consistent practitioner of spiritual ideals will reach the goal. Competitive, compulsive natures will rush to excel and generally find themselves repeating lessons and trials or stymied by little things that seemed of no importance earlier.

Certainly ego problems result from false values and distortions. These may come from either our outer life or experiences of astral phenomena. Meditators learn to discern and evaluate so they may pick their way carefully over a path ridden with psychological barriers, land mines lying in wait. Our ancient and hidden past waits to be cleared. If we are less compulsive, purification will occur more naturally and gradually. By consistent contact with higher energies and good spiritual guidelines, we will come to trust the process.

Symbols and Parables

> There is a thinking in primordial images—in symbols which are older than historical man, which have been ingrained in him from earliest times, and, eternally living, outlasting all generations, still make up the groundwork of the human psyche. It is only possible to live the fullest life when we are in harmony with these symbols; wisdom is a return to them. It is neither a question of belief nor of knowledge, but of the agreement of our thinking with the primordial images of the unconscious. They are the source of all our conscious thoughts, and one of these primordial thoughts is the idea of life after death. . . . They are indispensable conditions of the imagination; they are primary data.
> —C. G. Jung, *Modern Man in Search of a Soul*[1]

Becoming familiar with symbolic forms is part of the procedure for comprehending what the soul is able to access. *We must learn to think in symbols in order to perceive that which is cosmic in nature.* Abstract mind discovers patterns or divine designs. "God geometrizes," Pythagoras taught. We know recurring patterns and laws exist in nature; spiritual laws do as well. Great concepts are more easily handled with abstractions to guide us. Similarly, parables embody teaching tools to reach every level of understanding and offer solutions as we are challenged to simplify or exemplify great truths to evolving masses. Symbols and parables are easier to assimilate than "boxed" concepts and often bypass the rational mind of the listener, thus making a contribution in a subtle way.

> (The) old woman stands between the worlds of rationality and mythos. She is the knuckle bone on which these two worlds turn. This land between the worlds is that inexplicable place we all recognize once we experience it, but its nuances slip away and shape-change if one tries to pin them down, except when we use poetry, music, dance . . . or story.
>
> There is speculation that the immune system of the body is rooted in this mysterious psychic land, and also the mystical, as well as all archetypal images and urges including our God-hunger, our yearning for the mysteries, and all the sacred instincts as well as those which are mundane. Some would say the records of humankind, the root of light, the coil of dark are also here. It is not a void, but rather the place of the Mist Beings where things are and also are not yet, where shadows have substance and substance is sheer.
>
> —Clarissa Pinkola Estés
> *Women Who Run*
> *With the Wolves*[2]

Superconscious: undefined, no limit/collective consciousness of humanity.

Subconscious: personal field contains barriers, blocks, subconscious programming and beliefs, etc.

Ego/individuality, as focused awareness grows and expands through conscious inquiry.

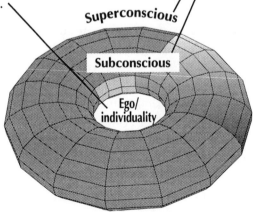

Figure 19. Wholeness. Living as a conscious soul increases the ego/individuality, our goal as we seek to expand the field of consciousness available to the divine Ego. Each time we affirm "I am the soul," we energize this goal. The affirmation strengthens spiritual influences hidden behind personality ego even in the non-awakened state; the energies magnify the ceaseless gnawing awareness that awaits out of sight. Desire for enlightenment expands, and right-remembrance is enhanced.

Concepts may be delivered to the conscious mind which desires data, while archetypes, symbols, and parables enrich the subconscious level to make change and correction, as well as provide positive reinforcement and processing for new ideas.

Lives adjust as a greater longing to fulfill our dharma, our reason for being, manifests: personal conditions may need modification to support our soul purpose—excuses dissolved, obligations fulfilled so obstacles lose their ability to block the soul in its coming to power. *The soul accepts no excuses; we cannot allow circumstances or environment to hinder our spiritual life.* They are only permitted to be overcome. Soul surmounts every obstacle, skillfully crafting each situation into a building block in the pyramid of high consciousness.

How to Recognize Success

As we live with focused awareness of ethics and choice, we will become better able to discern right-thought and right-action. We often think it is just that we have more common sense. We will probably experience expanded sensations immediately after our meditations, but such feelings of disorientation fade quickly; feelings of walking through our day "foggy" or "spacy" will vanish as well.

> *We must learn to think in symbols*
> *in order to perceive*
> *that which is cosmic in nature.*

With dedication to ethics and new spiritual understanding, our lives should reflect more stability, not monotonous or undifferentiated from others, for we are each unique in talent, but a composed and dignified balance of *rendering to Caesar the things that are Caesar's and to God the things that are God's.* We comprehend right-use of resources, able now to manage time, money, and our physical and our sexual natures.

We will probably discover an increased ability to see the unity of life more clearly, the wonder of synchronicity of events, and how the spiritual law of cause and effect manifests time and again. Moreover, we may see more explicitly how meditation symbols, our dreams, and impressions speak to us.

The focus on meditation increases our thirst to know and to be, and yet, at the same time, a great peacefulness enables us to allow the seeds we have planted to mature in nature's own good way.

As they continue to meditate, most spiritually motivated people simultaneously experience a deepening sense of responsibility for service; they realize they are significant to the whole of life. It is not a stressful feeling, but one of increased personal self-esteem. As we honor this sense of responsibility, we respectfully "phone home," tune in, listen, and respond, knowing we are an awakened part of the whole.

All these shifts in awareness help us transcend personality demands. We learn to work with others even as our personalities present their challenges. A certain detachment comes: from objects, people, and causes, from old perspectives. Old values subside; new values emerge: an intensified desire to serve, to radiate joy to others. Suddenly we find courage to stand for our own truth, clear and noble. Increasingly, we become all we can be, day by day.

The personality nature is increasingly energized by our inner powerhouse, charged by soul contact. Soul power, energy, and joy commission life. This is psychic energy, designed to bring about transformation. This magnetic, electrical force sets into motion the out-of-sight changes of transmutation. As we are taught in Agni Yoga, *prana,* the cosmic life force, is not assimilated into personality without psychic energy, the energy of the soul.

This energy is increased by meditation, service to a great cause, and heart-centered, impersonal love. It heals, purifies the emotional nature, organizes and assimilates mental energies of mind-stuff into expanded awareness or new levels of mind. All of this occurs behind the scenes as we continue our practice.

In spite of so much activity, a deepening sense of self simplifies the complexities of human life. We relax and allow life to reveal its secrets in its own time. We find we comprehend the deeper meaning of most happenings. Complicated matters are translated for us by wise ones into stories, symbols, and words. We rest in the sea of universal energy and comprehend more clearly that we are a part of it all. We have a deeper sense of our true Self.

What is happening now as a result of your meditation practice, particularly the procedures outlined in these lessons? The types of meditation you choose and your devoted practice of them will certainly affect what you experience now. Most likely you will begin thinking new thoughts and gaining fresh insights, many of which would not occur in years of ordinary secular living. You may be surprised to find depths within you did not know existed. For each person, experiences are quite different in form and character, but all have value because they reveal we are plumbing depths of consciousness of which we were not previously aware. Any or all of these changes will occur quite naturally.

I would like to share a seed-thought response I received November 11, 1992:

As I repeated the seed thought, "I Am that I AM," I became aware of an entire wall of mirror in front of me. When I saw myself in the mirror, my first thought was, *I am that I am.* The "I am of Creation" is mirrored in me; I, in fact, reflect the "I am of Creation."

As I followed that thought, I felt sadness in my heart, knowing I could not reflect the richness or the totality of the Creator. Upon realizing this disappointment and with a sense of inadequacy washing over me, I unexpectedly became the "great I AM" observing my sorrow.

As "i" experienced sadness and disappointment, the "great I AM" responded with the thought of how limiting was that sadness, that, in fact, by reacting sadly, I severed the very way I could be more like the Creator. As the "great I AM," I realized that it disappoints the Creator when we restrict ourselves by painful reaction to that which is natural.

I sat stunned. Then I chose to relax into the awareness again that "I am that I am" and I will be the best "I AM" possible. I resolve to mirror in my life all the good, the gracious, the divine awareness that I can, without judgment, for then I mirror the Creator to the best of my ability.

When we reach a plateau in meditation, we ask, "How is this seed-thought meaning being expressed in my life and in the lives of those around me?" or, "How can I see this quality more clearly and more broadly in everyday living?"

For some, a flow of beautiful language will come; others will better understand the seed-thought virtues and themes. Meditation opens new vistas, while, at the same time, we learn to live more fully and harmoniously. Some may find themselves beyond intellect, in a state of pure consciousness that reveals vast meanings which are inexpressible. Many unexpected blessings will come from and go beyond these.

Having contacted a dynamic serenity, meditation will become a part of your daily living, at least a portion of the time. Difficult tasks will seem easier, relationships less strained, fear and anger reduced. Reflect on and describe what has happened to you as a result of meditating. It may be quite different from others, and that, too, is good.

One seed thought or question often provides stimulation enough for several sessions. Encourage depth exploration by following the basic format and asking, "Is there another way to look at this seed thought?"

To reread what has been received in previous meditations stimulates the flow as, once again, we reconnect to both the ideas and the energy of the thought. When it begins to flow again, be pleased, and, again, just start writing.

Perhaps the length of time to meditate upon each seed thought needs clarification. We have suggested focusing on each seed thought for at least twenty minutes (not more than once each day) for fifteen sessions within a period of about thirty days. These numbers carry no magic; they are simply to allow for thorough exposure to the depths of meaning contained in each seed thought.

However, should you "run dry" before fifteen sessions are given to a particular seed thought, stay with it nevertheless, and send in your response at the end of the two weeks or so. Sometimes you will experience a significant breakthrough after several days of "nothing." If you do not complete fifteen sessions in thirty days, send your report at that time anyway. If you have difficulty, let us know. Some daily meditation, relaxation, or attunement is strongly recommended. The many benefits configuring off-stage may be hard to discern now, but time will reveal them.

Preparation for the "I Am the Soul" Meditation

Our birth is but a sleep and a forgetting
    The Soul that rises with us, our life's Star,
Hath elsewhere its setting,
    And cometh from afar.
Not in entire forgetfulness,
    And not in utter nakedness,
But trailing clouds of glory do we come
    From God, who is our home.

—William Wordsworth
from *Ode on the Intimations of Immortality*

To begin "I am the Soul" meditation, we prepare with devotional activity—reading, chanting, or prayer. As we turn our attention inward, we lift our focus to the soulstar overhead and draw its energy down to the heart to expand both caring and feeling. What is the soulstar? This symbol of a bright star represents the presence of the luminous soul (and solar angel) from which the personality has descended. This archetype continues to overlight and constantly reminds personality of its true nature and source of power.

With purposeful procedure, we set into motion two emotional activities: first, we focus upon the heart to prompt a flow of devotion; second, devotion leads us to adoration, igniting aspiration and lifting us into the highest level of our astral nature. Similarly, we engage in two mental processes: concentration and contemplation. All of these play a part, and yet we define "meditation" as that central experience of it all, the place of special contact.

As we stimulate heart, engage mind, and invoke soul, we seek to *know* in the light of this contact. Consistent practice results in increased sensory awareness in the body, especially if we concurrently use other practices of clearing blocks within the body. We allow emotions to expand, to be felt and cleared. We seek to develop new capabilities: "Let this mind be in you, which was also in Christ Jesus." (Philippians 2.5) The path of action for the Christ-centered is to live consciously with one another and to create a life of service. As we are increasingly illumined, that light of the Christ affects all our actions. A life reflecting higher consciousness results.

A Study: "I Am the Soul" Mantra[3]

I am the Soul,
and also love am I.
Above all else, I am
both will and fixed design.
My will is now to lift
the lower self into the light divine.
That light am I.

Therefore, I must descend
to where that lower self awaits,
awaits my coming.
That which desires to lift
and that which cries for lifting
are now at one.
Such is my will.

This mantra is related to the steps of growth that demonstrate a commitment to living as a disciple: to embrace transformation and transmutation. It is designed to move the consciousness from one level of perception about ourselves to another.

I am the soul, and also love am I acknowledges our true identity—powerful affirmations to etch upon our consciousness.

Above all else, I am both will and fixed design. The will is the creative power of the universe, focused to engender action. "Fixed design" affirms the cosmic pattern through which life energy flows, creating what we call "the Plan," not in a minute way but in the wholeness. The fixed design includes the nonself, the conscious, the mask of the personality, and the divine design through which life works (the seven bodies, the seven planes, the masculine/feminine). This phrase also refers to the instinctual nature, those patterns which have nothing to do with our intellect and are not possible to change (birth date, race, gender, parentage).

The life evolving upward through the kingdoms prepares to receive the spark that is being ignited—that is placement, fixed pattern, fixed design of the universe. Even by our wills we are not going to change it; "little will" cannot alter fixed design. When we affirm, "I am both will and fixed design," we recognize that part of us that participates in the greater plan for life.

When *my will is now to lift the lower self into the light divine,* the personality that has brought us to meditation is ready for discipline. We choose to adjust the personality nature to the light. We choose to place ourselves in posture to contact the divine Self.

That light am I. Designed to move our identity from the personality to the soul, the "I am," we affirm again our oneness with the divine; willingly, the true nature *must descend to where the lower self awaits.*

We move our focus from personality to soul, to the divine Self. Now, from the power of higher will of Self, we pour forth strength as a divine being, moving energy down to personality. The higher consciousness descends to where the lower self *awaits my coming,* to act through and upon the personality.

That which desires to lift and that which cries for lifting are now at one: soul and personality interlock. We invoke the power of the soul to lift our mundane, personality consciousness to a higher realm. Soul power is like a great magnet, and personalities are like bits and pieces of metal shavings. When the magnet is brought close, the shavings move to adhere to it. The cleaner the shavings, the more quickly they spring to the magnet. The personality responds naturally to oneness. Our work is to prepare our personalities so that the physical body, heart, and mind react eagerly when soul is activated.

Such is my will. That will is the united focus of personality will and soul will. This is the perfect pattern of the universe, aligning the lesser to the higher: "I am both will and fixed design." We affirm our humanness and our divine connection. This last line, "Such is my will," is the allegiance of all levels to work in perfect harmony. As we say it, an inner change is inevitable. It is gathering our will from every level of self and using its transmuting power to bring the union to the committed action of the moment. As we speak, we resolve to utilize the will of our every level to act as one.

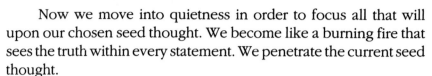

Now we move into quietness in order to focus all that will upon our chosen seed thought. We become like a burning fire that sees the truth within every statement. We penetrate the current seed thought.

Acting as divinity upon matter, the Christ-Within focuses upon the lower mental plane. This has a purifying effect, a clarity; that consciousness that *knows* gives its gift of knowledge. We invite its participation as we work "as if." The inner presence performs the "giving" role, and the personality receives. We seek transmutation, realizations, a revelation experience as the two entities interact.

Through understanding, the repetition of this mantra, and expansion of the self, we concentrate the energy of our various levels in one action: the integration, the release of barriers, and release of the identity that separates us from others. As these separations, barriers, and restrictions (veils) are thinned, an inner action occurs, and change happens within us.

Remember, you are not only changing on the personality level. This is part of the mystery: the personality level changes as it is transmuted, but also the soul begins to reveal its long-held purpose. The soul broadens its experience and dimensions as it presses into areas never before encountered.

The soul releases an outpouring of energy from its own resources to the personality being guided along the path of human initiation. Merging the two, soul and personality, is key, for neither can achieve without the other.

Follow the procedure outlined at the end of lesson 8, page 170, as you prepare for your seed-thought assignment. Now let us proceed to use "I am the Soul" as a seed thought. What additional awareness can we gain? We focus on the seed-thought process to capture our impressions: form, quality, purpose, and cause.

Assignment

> **Seed Thought: I am the Soul**

Our seed thought, "I am the Soul," challenges us to press into our true nature and to break free of personality's hold. We cry out to the higher level of our being, to the Masters and the holy ones to assist us in transferring our perspective to that of our true nature. We seek to know "I am the Soul" and to know what the soul knows.

Appendix

The Great Invocation

From the point of Light within the Mind of God
  Let light stream forth into the minds of men.
    Let Light descend on Earth.

From the point of Love within the Heart of God
  Let love stream forth into the hearts of men.
    May Christ return to Earth.

From the center where the Will of God is known
  Let purpose guide the little wills of men—
    The purpose which the Masters know and serve.

From the center which we call the race of men
  Let the Plan of Love and Light work out
    And may it seal the door where evil dwells.

Let Light and Love and Power restore the Plan on Earth.

Lead us, O Lord

Lead us, O Lord,
        from darkness to light,
        from the unreal to the real,
        from death to immortality,
        from chaos to beauty.   Amen.[3]

I Am the Soul

I am the Soul,
and also love am I.
Above all else, I am
both will and fixed design.
My will is now to lift
the lower self into the Light Divine.
That Light am I.
Therefore, I must descend
To where that lower self awaits,
awaits my coming.
That which desires to lift
and that which cries for lifting
Are now at one.
Such is my will.

Affirmation of the Disciple

I am a point of light within a greater Light.
I am a strand of loving energy within the stream of Love divine.
I am a point of Sacrificial Fire, focused within
the fiery Will of God.
        And thus I stand.
I am a way by which men may achieve.
I am a source of strength, enabling them to stand.
I am a beam of light, shining upon their way.
        And thus I stand.
And standing thus revolve
And tread this way the ways of men,
And know the ways of God.
        And thus I stand.

Afterword: A Clarion Call

Envisioning is a spiritual work offered to those ready to accept an invitation to restore the Plan on Earth. It hastens the manifestation of the seeker's own part, at the same time strengthening the many activities needed to make up the whole. World servers—disciples—work not for themselves alone, but align with the Holy Ones to fulfill humanity's role in planetary life.

A great need exists now for knowledgeable leaders and trained workers. We awake to new opportunities every day. The long-awaited time of high consciousness is advancing rapidly, and you and I have many roles to play. Envisioning consists of perceiving the subtle forces within our own nature guiding us toward our purpose, concurrently recognizing and respecting the efforts of other light workers.

Expansion of consciousness means we see more of life; we perceive, we intuit, we know in a new way. *It is for this that each soul incarnates.* Our inner nature longs to become whole. Of course, personality often suffers hurt. That is what causes the congealed balls of "stuff" that exist in the stream of life. In time, we will attract something to cause us to study and heal those blocks, freeing that stored energy for new endeavors and more positive use. In due time, we will address our confusions over issues—any issues. The universal laws of karma and reincarnation guarantee this.

While a resistance to the new is understandable, we need to face the causative issues; we need to determine how we would love to serve and how we could do so comfortably. When we are able to appreciate the laws of abundance and count our blessings, we will comprehend the greater picture. When we decline to be generous with whatever gifts we have, we are the losers. When we give generously to that which we love, it grows, and we benefit.

Desire attracts (in esoteric language we say, "magnetizes"). When we yearn to achieve a goal, we create a line of energy between ourselves and an image of the goal. The emotional charge draws us and the goal onto the same wave length, and as we energize the goal, it moves toward us as we move toward it. It becomes more feasible, then more probable as it gathers energy with which to manifest.

A number of energies are needed: focus, desire, drive, hope, strength, intention, reinforcement, encouragement, enthusiasm—to name a few. Role models, breakthroughs, and reassurance contribute to both the renewing of self and the manifestation of new possibilities. And new possibilities are life unfolding. Envisioning programs keep necessary energies flowing along the line of desired possibility whether we are focusing on our physical bodies, money for our personal life, or support for our group life.

Living through a time of transition means change is everywhere. Energy rises and falls; it shifts, swirls, and surges all about us. Visionaries recognize this resource is to be tapped for a loftier world view or it will feed the chaos created by fear and regress into the lower patterns of the past.

Each of us stands at a similar point of tension. We may direct our energy toward holding on to the past or creating an empowering future; most of us have to do some of both. We may need to forgive or release someone or something, at the same time asking hard questions about where we are now and how we envision the new we desire.

Humanity needs workers for the new future. What can you offer? Coworkers need one another and need to multiply themselves in the lives and work of many who will sustain what is only begun, those who feel called to "the Work," who wish to be a living, contributing part of it. Knowing our soul creates expressions that lead to high perspectives and aligns us to the purposes of our incarnation, many seekers come to realize an eclectic and ecumenical path is the right one for them.

The spiritual hierarchy—called "elder brothers" by some, "ascended masters" by others—provides an example for us all. Male and female, they contribute to the Great Plan under allegiance to the Christ—teacher of angels and of humanity. They must struggle, adapt, and re-form according to humanity's responses to guidance, perhaps their most difficult task. We remember many times we have had to adjust to the needs of others.

Even though thousands receive instruction in meditation and intuition, the Holy Ones still wait for humanity's consciousness to move forward, not casually or sporadically, but with dedication and transformation. While a few today are strongly committed, the call is for many to embrace a life of spirituality and form a reservoir of consciousness open and ready to carry humanity through the next challenging yet significant years.

Envisioning is a tool to assist each of us in participating in the transformation of our society. It is also a means of magnetizing others to take steps in devising ways of assisting humanity in its ascension. We are building a divine design in the etheric, as well as on the physical. Led by the Masters, we will love and serve. It is a noble work.

Endnotes

Lesson 1.

[1]H. Saraydarian, *The Science of Meditation* (Agoura, CA: Aquarian Educational Group, 1971).

[2]Vera Stanley Alder, *Fifth Dimension* (York Beach, ME: Samuel Weiser, Inc., 1993).

[3]Geoffrey Smith, "Meditation, the New Balm for Corporate Stress," *Business Week* (May 10, 1993).

[4]See recommended reading list at the end of the book.

[5]Bill King, Ph.D., past professor of psychology, St. Petersburg (Florida) Community College.

[6]Tarthang Tulku, *Time, Space, and Knowledge* (Berkeley, CA: Dharma Publishing, 1977).

[7]James N. Powell, *The Tao of Symbols* (New York: William Morrow and Company, Inc., 1982).

[8]Paraphrased from Corinne Heline, *Sacred Science of Numbers* (Marina del Ray, CA: DeVorss & Company, 1991).

[9]Paraphrased from Florence Campbell, *Your Days Are Numbered* (Marina del Ray, CA: DeVorss & Company, 1931).

Lesson 2.

[1]John White, *The Meeting of Science and Spirit* (New York: Paragon House, 1990).

[2]Ram Dass, *Journey of Awakening* (New York: Bantam Books, 1978).

[3]Haridas Chaudhuri, *Integral Yoga* (Wheaton, IL: Theosophical Publishing House, 1974).

[4]Richard Hittleman, *Guide to Yoga Meditation* (New York: Bantam Books, 1969).

[5]William Matthews, in the "Investment Advisory Newsletter" of *Sound Money Investor,* August 1989 (420 S. Orlando Ave., Winter Park, FL 32789).

[6]Guided meditations on tape: *Meditation Plus* and *Experience New Dimensions* are two sets of tapes by Carol E. Parrish-Harra, available through Village Bookstore, Sparrow Hawk Village, 22 Summit Ridge, Tahlequah, OK 74464. (918) 456-3421. (*Meditation Plus* should be used first.)

[7]Two Disciples, *Rainbow Bridge Techniques* (Danville, CA: The Triune Foundation, 1988, 3rd edition).

[8]*Coming to the Sunrise* is a set of tapes by Carol E. Parrish-Harra, available through Village Bookstore.

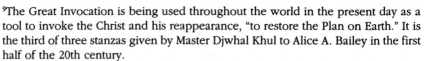

[9]The Great Invocation is being used throughout the world in the present day as a tool to invoke the Christ and his reappearance, "to restore the Plan on Earth." It is the third of three stanzas given by Master Djwhal Khul to Alice A. Bailey in the first half of the 20th century.

[10]*The Science of Meditation,* a booklet compiled from Alice A. Bailey materials by the Arcane School, 113 University Place, New York 10003, n.d.

[11]Lawrence LeShan, *How to Meditate* (New York: Bantam Books, 1974).

[12]Patricia Carrington, *Freedom in Meditation* (Garden City, NY: Anchor Press/Doubleday, 1978).

[13]Pandit Usharbudh Arya, *Superconscious Meditation* (Honesdale, PA: Himalayan International Institute, 1978).

[14]Roy Eugene Davis, *An Easy Guide to Meditation* (Lakemont, GA: CSA Press, 1978).

[15]Ethel Lombardi is president and founder of MariEl International and president of MariEl Foundation for Peace, Lockport, IL.

[16]The Mikel Institute and Center, Sunset Ridge Business Park, 5821 Cedar Lake Road, St. Louis Park, Minnesota 55416, (612) 546-7902.

[17]Vera Stanley Alder, *The Finding of the Third Eye* (Rider & Co., England, 1938; first American edition, Samuel Weiser, Inc., York Beach, ME, 1970; 16th printing, 1985).

[18]Manly P. Hall, *Self-Unfoldment by Disciplines of Realization* (Los Angeles: Philosophical Research Society, 1961).

[19]H. Saraydarian, *Cosmos in Man* (Agoura, CA: The Aquarian Educational Group, 1973).

Lesson 3.

[1]Alice A. Bailey, *The Light of the Soul* (New York, Lucis Publishing Co., 1955) is widely considered the most worthwhile translation and commentary on the Yoga Sutras of Patanjali.

[2]I highly recommend this reading material, available through CSA Press in Lakemont, Georgia 30552.

[3]*Psychosynthesis* (New York: Viking Press, 1971). Roberto Assagioli, 1888-1975, M.D., developer of and author of *Psychosynthesis.* He is referred to as "one of the masters of modern psychology in the line that runs from Freud through Jung and Maslow . . .(and) a colleague of all these men."

[4]Ken Wilber, *Eye to Eye* (Garden City, NY: Anchor Books, 1983).

[5]Ibid.

[6]Clarissa Pinkola Estés, *Women Who Run With the Wolves* (New York: Ballantine Books, 1992).

[7]Manly P. Hall, *Self-Unfoldment by Disciplines of Realization* (Los Angeles: Philosophical Research Society, 1961).

[8]Lawrence LeShan, *How to Meditate* (New York: Bantam Books, 1974).

[9]Bradford Smith, *Meditation: The Inward Art* (Philadelphia: Lippincott, 1963).

[10]Christmas Humphreys, *Concentration and Meditation* (Baltimore, MD: Penguin Books, 1969).

[11]Lama Anagarika Govinda, *The Significance of Meditation in Buddhism.* In Hanson, Virginia, *Approaches to Meditation* (Wheaton, IL: Theosophical Publishing House, 1973).

[12]Alice A. Bailey, *The Externalization of the Hierarchy* (New York: Lucis Publishing Co., 1957).

[13]Corinne Heline, *Mystery of the Christos* (Santa Monica, CA: New Age Bible and Philosophy Center, 1961).

[14]*Song of God*, the Bhagavad Gita with commentary by Swami Venkatesananda. (San Francisco, CA: The Chiltern Yoga Trust, revised 1984).

[15]*The Aquarian Gospel of Jesus the Christ,* by Levi (Marina del Rey, CA: DeVorss & Company, 12th printing, 1988).

[16]Vera Stanley Alder, *The Finding of the Third Eye* (York Beach, ME: Samuel Weiser, Inc., 16th printing, 1985).

Lesson 4.

[1]Harold H. Bloomfield, M.D., et al, *Transcendental Meditation—Discovering Inner Energy and Overcoming Stress* (New York: Dell Publishing Co., Inc., 1975).

[2]Jose Silva, *The Silva Mind Control Method* (New York: Simon and Schuster, 1977).

[3]Robert E. Ornstein, *Psychology of Consciousness* (San Francisco: Freeman, 1972).

[4](Vol. 1), by the Himalayan Institute of Yoga Science and Philosophy, 907 E. Camp McDonald Road, Prospect Heights, Illinois.

[5]A. H. Maslow, "A Theory of Human Motivation," *Psychological Review* 50 (1943).

Lesson 5.

[1]Bradford Smith, *Meditation: The Inward Art* (Philadelphia: Lippincott, 1963).

[2]C. Naranjo and R.E. Ornstein, *On the Psychology of Meditation* (New York: Penguin Books, 1976).

[3]Haridas Chaudhuri, *Integral Yoga* (Wheaton, IL: Theosophical Publishing House, 1974).

[4]Arcane School (from Alice A. Bailey works), 11th Floor, 113 University Place, New York, NY 10003, n.d.

[5]Roy Eugene Davis, *Teachings of the Masters of Perfection* (Lakemont, GA: CSA Press, 1979).

[6]Roy Eugene Davis, *Yoga Darsana: The Philosophy and Light of Yoga* (Lakemont, GA: CSA Press, 1976).

Lesson 6.

[1]Produced by Light of Christ Community Church singers, Sparrow Hawk Village; available through Village Bookstore, 22 Summit Ridge Dr., Tahlequah, OK 74464, (918) 456-3421.

[2]Torkom Saraydarian, *The Science of Meditation* (Sedona, AZ: Aquarian Educational Group, 1971).

[3]Carol E. Parrish-Harra, (Santa Monica, CA: IBS Press; now owned, copyrighted, and distributed by Sparrow Hawk Press, Tahlequah, OK).

[4]Gordon Davidson, The Sirius School, 5904 Madawaska Road, Bethesda MD 20816, 1993.

[5]The unfinished pyramid with the all-seeing eye in the capstone position (see a dollar bill!) suggests the United States will flourish when its leaders are guided by divine will.

[6]Alice Bailey materials.

[7]Alice Bailey materials.

[8]Two Disciples, *The Rainbow Bridge II: Link with the Soul—Purification* (Danville, CA: Rainbow Bridge Productions, 3rd Ed., 1988).

Lesson 7.

[1]Helena Petrovna Blavatsky, 1831-1891, born southern Russia, author and cofounder of the Theosophical Society with Col. Henry S. Olcott. "The basic tenets she boldly enunciated constitute the very essence of all occult doctrine. To begin to understand them is to begin to know her; and to know the doctrine she taught is to begin to know Truth." —Helen Todd and W. Emmett Small in the editorial foreword to *H. P. Blavatsky: The Mystery* by Gottfried de Purucker (San Diego, CA: Point Loma Publications, Inc., 1974).

[2]A paraphrase of John 14.12, "He who believes in me shall do the works which I do, and even greater than these things shall he do."

[3] Carol Parrish-Harra, *The Aquarian Rosary* (Tahlequah, OK: Sparrow Hawk Press, 1988), restated.

[4]Correspondence from Rev. Jan Skogstrom, Sept. 26, 1990, Minneapolis, MN.

[5]Alice A. Bailey, *A Treatise on White Magic* (New York: Lucis Publishing Co., 1987).

Lesson 8.

[1]M. Scott Peck, *Further Along the Road Less Traveled* (New York: Touchstone, 1993).

[2]See Guru R.H.H, *Talk Does Not Cook the Rice* (York Beach, ME: Samuel Weiser, Inc., 1982).

Lesson 9.

[1]C.G. Jung, *Modern Man in Search of a Soul* (New York: Harcourt, Brace & World, Inc., 1933).

[2]Clarissa Pinkola Estés, *Women Who Run With the Wolves* (New York: Ballantine Books, 1992).

[3]This ancient mantra, source unknown, is a transmuting device.

Suggested Additional Reading for Volume 1

In addition to the bibliography* herein, some of my favorite books to cultivate our spiritual sciences education and spiritual life are:

Regarding the three-brain concept:
Drawing on the Right Side of the Brain, Betty Edwards
Magical Child, Joseph Chilton Pearce
The Psychology of Consciousness, Robert Ornstein
Whole-Brain Thinking, Jacquelyn Wonder and Priscilla Donovan

Regarding numerology:
Numerology, Spiritual Light Vibrations, by Jeanne
Your Days Are Numbered—A Manual of Numerology for Everybody, Florence Campbell

Regarding spiritual science and initiations:
Ageless Wisdom, Torkom Saraydarian
The Coming of the Cosmic Christ, Matthew Fox
A Different Christianity, Robin Amis
Discipleship in the New Age, Volume II, Alice A. Bailey
The Finding of the Third Eye, Vera Stanley Alder
From Bethlehem to Calvary, Alice A. Bailey
The Gateway of Liberation, Mary Gray
Handbook to Higher Consciousness, Ken Keyes
The Initiation of the World, Vera Stanley Alder
The Masters and the Path, C. W. Leadbeater
Mystery of the Christos, Corinne Heline
The Science of Becoming Oneself, Torkom Saraydarian
The Science of Meditation, Torkom Saraydarian
In Search of the Primordial Tradition and the Cosmic Christ, John Rossner
Talks on Agni, Torkom Saraydarian
TheoSophia, Arthur Versluis
The Yoga of Christ, Ravi Ravindra

*Please see the bibliography for publishing information.

Bibliography

A Course in Miracles. Tiburon, CA: Foundation for Inner Peace, 1975.

Ainsworth, Stanley. *Positive Emotional Power*. Englewood Cliffs, NJ: Prentice-Hall, 1981.

Alder, Vera Stanley. *The Initiation of the World*. London, England: Rider & Company Limited, 1939.

____. *The Finding of the Third Eye*. 16th Printing. York Beach, ME: Samuel Weiser, Inc., 1985.

____. *Fifth Dimension*. York Beach, ME: Samuel Weiser, Inc., 1993.

Amis, Robin. *A Different Christianity*. Albany, NY: State University of New York, 1995.

Arya, Pandit Usharbudh. *Superconscious Meditation*. Honesdale, PA: Himalayan International Institute, 1978.

Assagioli, Roberto. *Psychosynthesis*. New York: Viking Press, 1971.

Bailey, Alice A. *Initiation, Human and Solar*. New York: Lucis Publishing Co. 1st Printing, 1922. 15th Printing, 1984.

____. *The Light of the Soul*. 1st Printing, 1927. 12th Printing, 1983.

____. *A Treatise on White Magic*. 1st Printing, 1934. 16th Printing, 1987.

____. *From Bethlehem to Calvary*. 1st Printing, 1937. 7th Printing, 1981.

____. *Glamour, A World Problem*. 1st Printing, 1950. 8th Printing, 1988.

____. *Discipleship in the New Age, Volume II*. 1st Printing, 1955. 7th Printing, 1986.

____. *The Externalization of the Hierarchy*. 1st Printing, 1957. 7th Printing, 1982.

____. *The Science of Meditation*. n.d.

Bloomfield, Harold H., M.D., et al. *Transcendental Meditation—Discovering Inner Energy and Overcoming Stress*. New York: Dell Publishing Co., Inc., 1975.

Brumgardt, Helen. *Contemplation*. Lakemont, GA: GSA Press, n.d.

Bucke, Richard Maurice. *Cosmic Consciousness*. New York: Citadel Press, 1970.

Campbell, Florence. *Your Days Are Numbered*. Marina del Ray, CA: DeVorss & Company, 1931.

Campbell, Joseph. *The Power of Myth*. New York: Doubleday, 1988.

Carrington, Patricia. *Freedom in Meditation*. Garden City, NY: Anchor Press/ Doubleday, 1978.

Chaudhuri, Haridas. *Integral Yoga*. Wheaton, IL: Theosophical Publishing House, 1974.

Davis, Roy Eugene. *How You Can Use the Technique of Creative Imagination*. Lakemont, GA: CSA Press, 1974.

____. Yoga Darsana: *The Philosophy and Light of Yoga*. Lakemont, GA: GSA Press, 1976.

____. *An Easy Guide to Meditation*. Lakemont, GA: GSA Press, 1978.

____. *The Teachings of the Masters of Perfection*. Lakemont, GA: GSA Press, 1979.

____. *The Science of Kriya Yoga*. Lakemont, GA: CSA Press, 1984.

de Purucker, Gottfried. *H. P. Blavatsky: The Mystery*. San Diego, CA: Point Loma Publications, Inc., 1974.

Edwards, Betty. *Drawing on the Right Side of the Brain*. Los Angeles: J. P. Tarcher, 1979.

Estés, Clarissa Pinkola. *Women Who Run With the Wolves*. New York: Ballantine Books, 1992.

Evans-Wentz, W.Y., Editor. *Tibetan Yoga and Secret Doctrines*. New York: Oxford University Press, 1967.

Fox, Matthew. *The Coming of the Cosmic Christ*. San Francisco: Harper & Row, 1988.

Frankl, Viktor E. *Man's Search for Meaning*. New York: E.P. Dutton, 1977.

Gibran, Kahlil. *The Prophet*. New York: Alfred A. Knopf, 103rd printing, 1979.

Goldsmith, Joel S. *The Art of Meditation*. New York: Harper and Row, 1956.

Goleman, Daniel. *The Varieties of Meditation*. New York: Pocket Books, 1963.

Govinda, Lama Anagarika. *The Significance of Meditation in Buddhism*. Wheaton, IL: Theosophical Publishing House, 1973.

Gray, Mary. *The Gateway of Liberation*. Tahlequah, OK: Sparrow Hawk Press, 1992.

Hall, Manly P. *Self-Unfoldment by Disciplines of Realization*. Los Angeles: Philosophical Research Society, 1961.

Heline, Corrine. *Mystery of the Christos*. Santa Monica, CA: New Age Bible and Philosophy Center, 1961.

____. *Sacred Science of Numbers*. Marina del Ray, CA: DeVorss & Company, 1991.

Hittleman, Richard. *Guide to Yoga Meditation*. New York: Bantam Books, 1969.

Humphreys, Christmas. *Concentration and Meditation*. Baltimore, MD: Penguin Books, l969.

Jampolsky, Gerald G. *Love Is Letting Go of Fear*. New York: Bantam Books, 1981.

Jeanne. *Numerology, Spiritual Light Vibrations*. Salem, OR: Your Center for Truth Press, 1987.

Jung, Carl Gustav. *Modern Man in Search of a Soul*. New York: Harcourt, Brace & World, Inc., 1933.

____. *Man and His Symbols*. New York: Doubleday, 1964.

Keyes, Ken. *Handbook to Higher Consciousness*. Berkeley, CA: Living Love Center, 1975.

Krishnamurti, Jiddu. *The World of Peace*. Meetings in Brockwood Park. England: Krishnamurti Foundation Limited, 1985.

Lamsa, George M., Translator. The Holy Bible from the Ancient Eastern Text, containing the Old and New Testaments, translated from the Aramaic of the Peshitta. Philadelphia, PA: A. J. Holman, 1933.

Lauback, Frank. *Channels of Spiritual Power*. Westwood, NJ: Fleming H. Revel Co., 1954.

Leadbeater, C. W. *The Masters and the Path*. Adyar, Madras, India: Theosophical Publishing House. lst Printing, 1925. 10th Reprint, 1973.

Leichtman, Robert R. and Carl Japikse. *Active Meditation*. Columbus, OH: Ariel Press, 1982.

LeShan, Lawrence. *How to Meditate*. New York: Bantam Books, 1974.

Levi. *The Aquarian Gospel of Jesus the Christ*. Marina del Ray, CA: DeVorss & Company, 12th printing, 1988.

Maltz, Maxwell. *Psycho-Cybernetics*. New York: Pocket Books, 1969.

Maslow, A. H. "A Theory of Human Motivation," *Psychological Review* 50, 1943.

Matthews, William. "Investment Advisory Newsletter" of *Sound Money Investor*, August 1989.

Meditation in Christianity, Volume I. Prospect Heights, IL: Himalayan Institute of Yoga Science and Philosophy, n.d.

Metzner, Ralph. *Opening to Inner Light*. Los Angeles: Jeremy P. Tarcher, 1986.

Naranjo, Claudio and Robert E. Ornstein, *On the Psychology of Meditation*. New York: Penguin Books, 1976.

Ornstein, Robert E. *Psychology of Consciousness*. San Francisco: W. H. Freeman and Company, 1972.

Parker, William and Elaine St. John. *Prayer Can Change Your Life*. New York: Prentice Hall Press, 1957.

Pearce, Joseph Chilton. *Evolution's End*. New York: Harper Collins, 1993.

____. *Magical Child*. 6th edition. New York: Bantam Books, 1986.

Peck, M. Scott. *Further Along the Road Less Traveled*. New York: Touchstone, 1993.

Pelletier, Kenneth R. *Mind as Healer/Mind as Slayer*. New York: Dell Publishing Co., 1977.

Powell, James N. *The Tao of Symbols*. New York: William Morrow and Company, 1982.

Ram Dass, Baba. *Journey of Awakening*. New York: Bantam Books, 1978.

Ravindra, Ravi. *The Yoga of the Christ*. Longmead, England: Element Books Limited, 1990.

Roerich, Helena. *Leaves of Morya's Garden*. New York: Agni Yoga Society, 3rd printing, 1953.

____. *Letters*. New York: Agni Yoga Society. *Volume 1*, 1954. *Volume II*, 1967.

Rossner, John. *In Search of the Primordial Tradition and the Cosmic Christ.* St. Paul, MN: Llewellyn Publications, 1989.

Russ, Michael. *The Why and How of Meditation.* Washington, DC: Millennium Publishing House, 1975.

Sadhu, Mouni. *Meditation.* North Hollywood, CA: Wilshire Book Co., 1972.

Saraydarian, H. (Torkom). *The Science of Becoming Oneself.* Sedona, AZ: The Aquarian Educational Group, 1969.

_____. *The Science of Meditation.* Sedona, AZ: Aquarian Educational Group, 1971.

_____. *Cosmos in Man.* Agoura, CA: Aquarian Educational Group, 1973.

_____. *Talks on Agni.* Sedona, AZ: Aquarian Educational Group, 1987.

_____. *The Ageless Wisdom.* West Hills, CA: T.S.G. Publishing Foundation, Inc., 1990.

Silva, Jose. *The Silva Mind Control Method.* New York: Simon and Schuster, 1977.

Smith, Bradford. *Meditation: The Inward Art.* Philadelphia, PA: Lippincott, 1963.

Smith, Geoffrey. "Meditation, the New Balm for Corporate Stress." *Business Week,* May 10, 1993.

Song of God, The Bhagavad Gita, commentary by Swami Venkatesananda. San Francisco: The Chiltern Yoga Trust, revised 1984.

Tulku, Tarthang. *Time, Space, and Knowledge.* Berkeley, CA: Dharma Publishing, 1977.

Two Disciples. *Rainbow Bridge Techniques.* 3rd edition. Danville, CA: The Triune Foundation, Rainbow Bridge Productions, 1988.

Versluis, Arthur. *TheoSophia.* Hudson, NY: Lindisfarne Press, 1994.

White, John. *The Meeting of Science and Spirit.* New York: Paragon House, 1990.

Wilber, Ken. *Eye to Eye.* Garden City, NY: Anchor Books, 1983.

Wonder, Jacquelyn and Priscilla Donovan. *Whole-Brain Thinking.* New York: Ballantine Books, 1984.

Wood, Ernest. *Yoga.* Baltimore, MD: Penguin Books, 1973.

Yogananda, Paramahansa. *Autobiography of a Yogi.* Los Angeles: Self-Realization Fellowship, 1946.

_____. *Metaphysical Meditations.* Los Angeles: Self-Realization Fellowship, 1982.

TAPES

Tapes designed as aids to the Meditation Course given by Carol E. Parrish-Harra are available through the Village Bookstore, Sparrow Hawk Village, 22 Summit Ridge Drive, Tahlequah, OK 74464:

Guided meditations on tape: *Meditation Plus* (to be used first) and *Experience New Dimensions.*

Coming to the Sunrise. Purification meditations on tape. Very powerful—follow directions carefully.

LCCC Sings, by the Light of Christ Community Church singers.

Sancta Sophia Seminary

A Contemporary Mystery School
How It Came to Be

I n 1982, Carol Parrish was revealed to the greater public by author Ruth Montgomery in the best-selling *Threshold to Tomorrow*. The book elaborated upon Carol's near-death experience, her remarkable psychic and spiritual abilities, and her current role as a messenger in the new age.

Just previously, Carol had received spiritual guidance to move the school she had established in 1978 from Florida to a specified, remote location in the beautiful Ozark foothills of eastern Oklahoma.

Today, in addition to her personal teaching of Sancta Sophia students, Carol is academic dean and oversees seminary classes, faculty, and advisors. She continues to minister at Light of Christ Community Church and has published widely acclaimed books and audio-cassette programs. She is a highly sought international speaker and world traveler.

Spiritually Charged Location Enhances Growth

The magnificent wooded 400-acre mountaintop setting where Carol was inspired to build Sparrow Hawk Village is also the home of Sancta Sophia Seminary. This spiritual community which provides a supportive environment for the practice of ethical living was founded by Reverend Parrish, her husband, Charles C. Harra, and her friend, Reverend Grace B. Bradley.

The village is a harmonious environment of fifty privately owned homes, office buildings, church, and wellness center. It has wooded homesites, lovely gardens, and a sophisticated infrastructure. Villagers are self-supporting people who live, learn, meditate, and worship together.

The church sanctuary is centered on a vortex of special energies created by a star-shaped convergence of Earth ley lines. This creates a unique enclosure of spiritual energies which enhance the synergy of living, learning, and personal growth for faculty, students, and villagers. It is a sacred place which helps individuals to heal and make their lives whole. Very importantly, the spiritual vortex provides an environment for the preparation and training of initiates in spiritual vocations.

How the Program Creates Personal Transformation

A combination of off-campus, home-study, and residential program forms the basis of participation in both graduate and undergraduate studies. The focal point of every student's program is a unique transformational process guided by a master teacher, Dean Parrish, together with skilled, dedicated faculty, advisors, tutors, counselors, and healers.

The process is integrative. It begins with selected study and meditation techniques tailored to the disciple's personal goals. Month-by-month, an individually assigned advisor offers spiritual mentoring in telephone sessions, personal meetings, and by correspondence. The entire process is catalyzed during periodic class sessions when students visit to enjoy the spiritually charged atmosphere of the campus at Sparrow Hawk.

Five Levels of Certification Available

The distinctive process of home study, meditation, spiritual guidance, and periodic classes prepares students for planetary service on one of five paths.

First, Practitioners earn certification as well-prepared lay ministers in counseling, spiritual healing, and teaching. Second, Teachers of Esoteric Philosophy become educators for the new paradigms of spirituality now emerging around the planet. Third, ordination prepares ministers in Esoteric Christianity to bring the true Ageless Wisdom into both metaphysical and mainstream settings around the world. Light of Christ Community Church ordinations are endorsed by the International Council of Community Churches.

Additionally, the graduate school offers two levels of certification to a limited enrollment. For students with the requisite background, commitment, and high creativity, individually designed programs lead to one of several master's or doctoral degrees.

All programs are moderate in cost.

For More Information

Do you seek to serve as a healing practitioner, minister, counselor, or teacher? Would you like to earn an advanced degree? Sancta Sophia programs can prepare you to contribute as an awakened leader in the era of enlightenment we are entering.

If you would like more information, you are invited to call the Registrar at (800) 386-7161, or write to Sancta Sophia Seminary, 11 Summit Ridge Drive-Dept. 33, Tahlequah, OK 74464. If you wish, you may request the name of the affiliated center, church, or class nearest you. We would be most happy to hear from you.

Books and Tapes for Spiritual Growth

Please send the following books:

Quantity		Price each	Totals
_____	Adventure in Meditation—Spirituality for the 21st Century, Vol. I — *a meditation guide to achieve soul infusion, by Carol E. Parrish-Harra, Ph.D.*	$17.95	_____
_____	The New Dictionary of Spiritual Thought – *1,100 definitions of esoteric and spiritual concepts, by Rev. Carol E. Parrish-Harra, Ph.D.*	$14.95	_____
_____	The Mystical, Magical, Marvelous World of Dreams – *a concise guide to dream interpretation, by Wilda B. Tanner*	$14.95	_____
_____	Do You Speak Astrology? *great for astrology beginners, by Doe Donovan*	$12.95	_____
_____	The Book of Rituals – *to create personal & planetary transformation, by Rev. Carol E. Parrish-Harra, Ph.D.*	$14.95	_____
_____	The New Age Handbook on Death and Dying – *excellent resource for comfort & guidance, by Rev. Carol E. Parrish-Harra, Ph.D.*	$10.95	_____
_____	The Gateway of Liberation – *classic writings on the Ageless Wisdom, by Mary Gray*	$10.95	_____
_____	Genesis: Journey into Light – *an esoteric interpretation, by Rev. Sarah Leigh Brown*	$ 7.95	_____
_____	Messengers of Hope – *a personal account of a transformative journey, by Rev. Carol E. Parrish-Harra (autobiography)*	$ 7.95	_____

Please send the following teaching tapes by Carol E. Parrish-Harra:

Adventure in Awareness – *Ageless Wisdom concepts & teachings:*

		Price	Totals
_____	I - Breadth of Esoteric Teachings (12 90-min. tapes)	$60.00	_____
_____	II - Awakening Our Inner Consciousness (12 90-min. tapes)	$60.00	_____
_____	III - Toward Deeper Self-Realization (12 90-min. tapes)	$60.00	_____
_____	Meditation Plus – *12 meditation techniques for spiritual growth (6 tapes)*	$30.00	_____
_____	Coming to the Sunrise – *advanced meditation for self-purification (4 tapes)*	$25.00	_____
_____	Energy Ecstasy *(book used with "Sunrise" Tapes)*	$12.95	_____
_____	Healing – *realize your own healing potential & how to use it (6 tapes)*	$30.00	_____
_____	New Age Christianity – *discover the Christ-Within (6 tapes)*	$30.00	_____
_____	Experience New Dimensions – *techniques for psychic development (6 tapes)*	$35.00	_____
_____	The Aquarian Rosary – *stimulate heart & mind to greater love (2 tapes)*	$12.95	_____
_____	The Aquarian Rosary (book)	$10.95	_____
_____	Meditation & Group Work for the 21st Century (2 tapes)	$15.95	_____
_____	Reincarnation & Karma (2 tapes)	$15.95	_____

Subtotal _____

☐ I am interested in knowing more about **Sancta Sophia Seminary.** Please send additional information.

Shipping and Handling
($2.50 first item, $.75 each additional) _____

TOTAL ENCLOSED *Payment by:* Check ☐ Visa ☐ MasterCharge ☐ Discover ☐ _____

Name_____
  (please print)

Address_____

_____Daytime Phone_____

Card #_____Exp. Date_____

Signature_____

VILLAGE BOOKSTORE
22 Summit Ridge Drive, Dept. 33
Tahlequah, OK 74464
For phone orders, call 800-386-7161

Books on Suggested Additional Reading list (page 207) also available